MAKING SCRIPTURE WORK

A practical guide to using Scripture in the local church

Christine Dodd

GEOFFREY
CHAPMAN

Geoffrey Chapman
An imprint of Cassell Publishers Ltd
Artillery House, Artillery Row
London SW1P 1RT

First published 1989

ISBN 0-225-66524-7

British Library Cataloguing in Publication Data

Dodd, Christine
    Making scripture work
    1. Christian church. Parish life.
    Use of Bible
    I. Title
    259

Typesetting by RP Typesetters

Printed and bound in Great Britain at
The Camelot Press plc, Southampton

Contents

Introduction

To
Father Gerald
in gratitude

Chapter 1

SCRIPTURE TODAY

Introduction

'I know nothing about the Bible. I have a feeling that I am missing out on something wonderful but no-one has ever opened up its contents to me or helped me to understand what it says. All I've had is an experience at school which made me think that the Scriptures are boring and irrelevant. It's a shame really because I'm sure they should be important to me.'

★

In *Dei Verbum*, one of the documents of the Second Vatican Council, the Church highlights the importance of reading the Scriptures and their place in the life of the Church. It is through them that God speaks, and *Dei Verbum* stresses that 'in the sacred books, the Father who is in heaven comes lovingly to meet his children and talks with them.' (*Dei Verbum*, 21). Unfortunately, for many people the experience of the Father meeting his children with great love in the Scriptures has never happened. In every parish one could hear similar comments to the one above. Such remarks sadly show that many Christians feel the need for access to the Bible as a way of experiencing God's presence but that they lack the direction and help to go about it. It is the aim of this book to help people in a practical way to discover for themselves the riches which lie within the pages of their Bibles.

This book is a practical one. It is about the 'how' of using the Scriptures. Its aim is twofold. Firstly to encourage individuals, some perhaps for the first time, to meet the Father in his Word and secondly to give practical help to parishes to enable this to happen. The book is also designed to encourage the whole parish community to discover in the Scriptures a way of guidance for its life. As such, it is aimed at leaders in a parish who would like to see Scripture given a more central role in the life of the whole community. It is for those who believe the Bible is important within the parish but would like some ideas about how to get things going and some guidelines about what to avoid. For this reason, the scope of this volume is wider than just how to use the Bible in the liturgy or in small groups. It tries to show how the Scriptures can be a source of nourishment throughout the whole range of parish activities, whether it is with children or young people, with the academic or non-academic, with pastoral care or with study groups.

It is because this book is aimed at using Scripture in a practical way within the parish that it will look in particular at how to approach the Bible creatively and at the range of opportunities open for work with Scripture. Above all, it will give many examples and comments which hopefully will enable you to compose your own programmes for both individual use and groups within the parish.

Finally, a word of warning. This book is not a blueprint for using Scripture in the parish. It should not be used (or even thought of) as such. Nor should the examples given in it be taken as perfect. They are *examples*. They give ideas of methods which can be used but they are a way of approach rather than a master guide. The key to successful use of Scripture in the parish is *always* to adapt. And then go on adapting! Sensitively adapting any material you decide to use to suit your own needs and situation will ensure that the method remains a tool in your hands and never becomes more important than the Word of God it seeks to clarify.

For years now I have been engaged in working with individuals, groups and communities who want a life-giving method of reading the Bible; a method that is relevant to the rest of their lives. This book is an outcome of that work with others.

■ WHY SCRIPTURE?

'Why Scripture?' may seem a strange question. After all, we know why Scripture is important. It is the Word of God, a record of our rich heritage; the story of God's dealings with his people. We believe that through the pages of the Bible God continues to communicate with us and that through them we continue to hear him speak. It is through Scripture that we can be challenged, guided and comforted. It is our Book. This is what we say we believe; so why ask the question 'Why Scripture?'.

The question is, I believe, important for three primary reasons. Firstly, it forces us to examine afresh our attitude to the Bible. What do we really think when we open the pages or when we discuss a passage together? What do we think, deep down, the Bible is for? Secondly, it forces us to examine afresh how we use the Scriptures. What we believe it is *for* will profoundly affect the *way* we use it and the way we handle it. Thirdly, asking the question, 'Why Scripture?' forces us to look seriously at what we believe about God: about how he communicates with us and what sort of God he reveals himself to be. So we need to look at the question seriously, for unless we do we may engage in all sorts of wonderful and exciting methods without ever getting to the heart of the matter. Let us then look at the three areas the question forces us to examine.

Attitudes to the Bible

For some people the question, 'Why Scripture?' is not one they would ask. It is just not important. Their attitude to the Bible is one of mystification. It has either become irrelevant for them or was never relevant in the first place. The Bible seems far removed, dealing with questions they do not ask, stemming from a culture with which they have little contact. For other people the exact opposite is true. For them Scripture is meaningful and relevant. It speaks to them of God's involvement in their world and points the way towards an answer to many of life's questions. They know the answer to the question, 'Why Scripture?'. For the vast majority of people within our churches there is a middle path. Most, deep down, believe that this *is* the Word of God, so it should be important; but most are also confused about how God speaks through it. They find it difficult to see how words, written so long ago, can be of much relevance to a modern twentieth-century person. They are often muddled rather than enlightened by the work of Biblical scholarship. They are confused about how much of the Bible can be said to be historically true and the value of those parts of it which are not; about how much they should accept on trust and how much they can question critically what they read. They feel a certain sense of guilt and that they don't have much faith if they question what they have been told is the very Word of God.

In many years of handling Scripture with individuals and with groups I have come to the conclusion that the most important starting point is to deal with this very confusion. People need help to know how to handle the text. They need help in knowing what to do with Scripture, how to approach it and what questions to ask of it. Helping people handle the text usually means helping them to answer that one big question that is uppermost in many of their minds: is it true? Work with Scriptures usually only takes off when this question has been sorted out. Unless we address ourselves to it confusion, disappointment and often apathy will be the result. For this reason we shall deal with this crucial question at length here before we look at the practical ways of opening the Bible for people.

The remainder of this first section on attitudes to the Bible is by Father John Ryan of St Marie's Cathedral, Sheffield. I am grateful to him for the way he helps us look in greater depth at the question, 'Is it true?' and at how we might work towards an answer. As Father Ryan points out, the 'is it true?' question is often equivalent to the 'did it happen?' question. People want to know whether the stories, the incidents recorded and the words as set down actually happened. Making Scripture work for people will not happen for many if we do not tackle this matter at the outset.

"The Truth of the Bible

"I have a minor speech defect. I roll my 'r's. A slight affliction that would scarcely be worth comment except for the name I inherited from my parents. I remember when I was quite little, six or seven I think, I went to the Junior Library for the first time. A vast universe of knowledge was opening up before me. I was entering a new world of encyclopaedias and pop-up picture books. An exciting moment in a little boy's life. I handed the librarian the card I had been given at school. 'And what's your name?' she asked sweetly. 'John Ryan,' I responded eagerly. 'Lyons,' she repeated erroneously and ran through her card index. Perplexed, she turned back. 'What did you say your name was?' 'John Ryan,' I replied uncertainly. 'Riley,' she affirmed apologetically and . . . drew a second blank. A queue had now formed. Firmness entered her voice as she repeated her question. Colour rose in my cheeks as I stammered my replies. 'Nylon?' she queried. 'Iron?' she ventured. By now I was bright crimson, tears were forming in the corners of my eyes and the queue was getting agitated. 'Could you spell it?' she asked to break the deadlock. I sniffled through the response: 'R...Y...A..N.' 'Ryan,' she exclaimed, 'why didn't you say that?' And she gave me a look, the sort of look we reserve for the demented. I didn't want the library tickets. I didn't want to enter the world of knowledge or go into the library ever again. I knew, how I knew, that the world is a wicked, horrible place, and worse, I knew that I was imperfect, inadequate. I couldn't even talk properly."

That story is one I use in many contexts, teaching and preaching. It can be directed to make a variety of points. Any power and appeal the story has comes, no doubt, from its being a true story, one we can readily associate with. We have all suffered such embarrassments and been made brutally aware of our inadequacies.

However, if you were to see a video tape of my childhood you would not see an episode exactly as I have narrated it, nor would you hear a conversation exactly as I have recorded it. I can point to discrepancies in the story: children did not join the library in the way described, and for me to go anywhere on my own at that age was unthinkable. No doubt there was an embarrassing episode in a library, but that was one of dozens, even hundreds of embarrassing situations when I said my name and the hearer misheard: situations which recur today. Even now I will use a variety of descriptions of myself to say who I am without announcing my surname, and if I cannot avoid giving my full name I quickly follow it with a spelling.

What we have in this story is the distilled essence of many embarrassments which has been moulded by the story-teller into a tale that, he hopes, will convince, grip, amuse and with which the listener will be able to associate. Is my story true? If this question means 'Is this story an accurate description of an encounter that took place in a particular location at a particular time?' then the answer is no. But is this always what we mean when we ask 'Is the story true?' The accurate retelling of one such incident might be true and would probably be extremely boring. Tolerating some discrepancies for the sake of the story and polishing the dialogue gives the story its power and appeal. Then the story is no longer just about a little boy who couldn't say his name, but is a story that speaks to everyone who has publicly been made aware of their imperfections. The story can then rightly be said to be profoundly true.

Truth and Falsehood

A story can be true while containing errors of fact and inconsistencies, provided that the intention of the story-teller was to tell a story that revealed truth rather than a story which tells of what actually happened. If we are giving evidence in court then we must do the latter. If we are teaching children to do good and avoid evil we will probably want to do the former. Thus the fables of Aesop, when they are seen as moral exhortations, are true, even though animals cannot speak. The legends of King Arthur are true, regardless of whether or not he ever existed, if they are understood to be stories which deal with the great themes of love and nobility, justice and death. In neither case would we say that they relate what actually happened somewhere at some time and we would surely feel that it would be inappropriate to say they are 'untrue' or 'lies'. So we make a special category for them and call them 'Fables' and 'Legends'.

That the question of truth and falsehood is more complicated than deciding 'did it really happen this way?' is further illustrated by returning to our public library. The shelves are clearly labelled: FICTION A-B; SCIENCE; GEOGRAPHY; HISTORY; BIOGRAPHY; LITERATURE; REFERENCE etc. Each book in each section is in some sense true. Certainly we would not say that any book was false, except for one or two autobiographies perhaps. But is each book true in the same way? Imagine an alien visitor to our local library who, like *Star Trek*'s Mr Spock, thinks entirely logically and who thinks that truth is only that which is the case. 'Where do I find true books?' he asks. 'They are all true' responds the librarian. 'We don't keep false books here.' He walks around. He picks up a book on computer programming. 'Good,' he thinks, beginning to feel at home, 'primitive but quaint.' He walks further. 'FICTION A-B,' he reads, and picks up *Watership Down*. 'Animals on this planet can speak,' he naturally concludes. He moves on. *The History Plays* by W. Shakespeare catch his eye. 'Strange,' he reflects, 'at a certain time past all the people of England spoke in blank verse.' Confused, he retires.

Truth is expressed and communicated in many different ways. The scientist seeks to express truth in one way; the artist and musician in other ways; the writer in yet other ways. And the way we will judge the truth of the writer will depend on the type of writing in which he or she is engaged.

The Truth of Scripture

That truth is communicated in a variety of ways is an uncontroversial assertion except in one context: a context in which intelligent, broadminded people of renowned commonsense find their eyes glaze over and narrow to a fixed and rigid stare. The rich and colourful landscape of truth drains to one monochromatic question, 'Did it happens as it says — yes or no?' There is no middle ground. When does this myopic rigidity set in? When they open the pages of the Bible.

I firmly believe that the Bible is the inspired Word of God, and that it is true. I believe that 'all Scripture is inspired by God and is profitable for teaching, for reproof, for correction, and for training in righteousness' (2 Tim 3:16). But I believe that the same rich notion of truth and the manifold forms of communicating truth apply to the Bible as to all other aspects of life and literature. The Bible is not a single, homogeneous work but a collection of books, a virtual library. It contains many different types of literature: story, poetry, law, prophecy, apocalyptic writing, parable, biography, sermon, letter . . . Are we to read these and judge their truth by using exactly the same criteria? Are we only to ask 'Did it happen?' to all these forms of literature? If we do we will reach some very strange conclusions: conclusions which require us to go to tortuous lengths in their defence. Thus expeditions are sent to Mount Ararat to scour its slopes for remains of Noah's Ark. The seven seas are searched to discover a large sea-monster in whose belly a man could live for seventy-two hours. The alternative is less strenuous: to accept that in neither of these cases are we dealing with historical reporting. In the story of the Flood we are dealing with *myth* — mankind's way of coming to an understanding of himself and of his place in the world by telling stories of beginnings. We find similar stories in every ancient culture. In the story of Jonah we are dealing with *parable* — a story which dramatically illustrates how God's mysterious purpose will not be thwarted. So, we must be careful not to transpose our modern understanding of the historian's method onto an ancient culture that had no desire to record history in our way.

In ancient Israel history was what we remembered and retold. What was remembered was what was important and what was important was what reinforced the self-understanding of the people. History remembered reinforced their understanding of their identity, their unity, their unique place as a nation. The stories that were handed down told how God, the Lord of history, was involved with his chosen people, giving them their unique identity and place in the world and in history. This does not mean that there are no accurate reminiscences in the Old Testament; far from it. But this was not the primary purpose of the story-telling and subsequent writing. As in my story at the beginning, the primary purpose was to reveal truth, not to tell it as it was in every detail. The Old Testament contains numerous discrepancies and inconsistencies. Stories were modified and handed on in various forms. But this does not mean they are untrue. Harry Williams in his autobiography *Some Day I'll Find You* (Collins/Fount, 1984) remembers teaching three rigid fundamentalists at Cambridge. He had them in sequence for a tutorial one afternoon a week. He pointed out to one of them that we find in Genesis three very similar stories: Abraham passes his wife off as his sister, first to Pharaoh, then to Abimelech, King of Gerar; later Isaac does the same thing with his wife, again to Abimelech. Williams suggested that here we have three versions in different traditions of the same story. 'Not at all,' came the reply, 'it was a favourite joke of Abraham's and his son shared his sense of humour.'

The approach epitomised by these students not only is grounded in a narrow notion of truth but also needs to find absolute truth in every statement. However, the Old Testament holds at times contradicting views. For instance, in some passages life after death is flatly denied (Ps 39:14; Job 7:8; 7:21); in other places existence after death is in the non-personal shadow world of Sheol (Ps 115:17; Job 38:12); a more personal view of the hereafter is affirmed in other texts (Ps 16:10; 49:16; 2 Macc 12:43-45). There was a development of thought through the Old Testament which is reflected in these passages. The truth which the Bible affirms cannot be judged from any particular text in isolation. Rather the question of truth is answered by the Bible as a whole.

The Inspiration of Scripture

The fundamentalist-literalist interpretation of the Bible follows from a particular understanding of inspiration — how the Bible came to be written and the role of God as its author. This approach argues that God is the principal author of the Bible; he cannot make any mistakes; therefore the Bible must be literally true in whole and in part. It is right that the role of God in the creation of the Bible is given due prominence, but this must not be at the cost of undervaluing the part played by the various human authors. God made human beings 'in his image and likeness' (Gen 1:26), to be his partner in dialogue. Is it credible that God would give mankind the distinctively human faculties of intellect and will, creative and artistic abilities, and then suspend them, relegating individuals to the level of automatons, playing the part of scribe or secretary to his dictation? Somehow a balance must be struck which affirms both the involvement of God and the participation of his people. The Bible is truly the Word of God and truly the words of humans. It is the work of God and the work of human hands. Its coming into being was part of a human

11

process, involving at times individuals, at times whole communities. It evolved through many stages before reaching its final form. This process was guided by the hand of God so that the final form is the product of a partnership, the action of God and the product of human striving: truly human words which communicate the divine message to be heard in faith. As human the Scriptures are limited and conditioned by time and place, but as Word of God they are able to speak to people of every age and place and reveal God's truth to them.

Biblical Criticism

Biblical scholars have developed different approaches to studying the text. If we look at the Gospels we can see what these are and see their value. They can help us see the richness of truth that lies in the pages of our Bibles.

During his public ministry Jesus taught the crowds and privately instructed his disciples. It seems likely that his method of instruction was the customary rabbinic style; he would announce the teaching and the disciples would learn it by heart. After the Resurrection the disciples taught what they had learnt at the feet of their Master and what they had heard him teach the crowd. No doubt they demonstrated the authority of this teaching by describing the wonderful things they had seen Jesus do: his healings and exorcisms.

After the death of Stephen the young Church in Jerusalem suffered persecution. Many Christians fled, taking the new teaching into the Diaspora, the Jewish communities spread round the Mediterranean, and to the Gentiles. The stories and the teachings were used in different contexts in the life of the various communities, in preaching and exhortation, in liturgical celebrations, in instruction and catechesis. They would be moulded and adjusted to suit their purpose, and detail extraneous to that purpose would be dropped. Where Jesus told a story is usually less important than what he said, so the inessential detail about place is forgotten. Thus what was remembered and passed on in the tradition was the heart of the teaching, suited to its new purpose, and devoid of any local colour.

The stories and sayings were passed on by word of mouth. Blocks of teachings would have been formed, linked not chronologically in the ministry of Jesus but by a common word or idea which made them more readily memorable. Each local community would have sayings and stories in common with other communities, though not necessarily adapted to the same purpose in the life of the Church. No doubt some churches preserved some teachings that were lost to others.

The study of these individual sayings or stories (*pericopes*) which attempts to identify the use of the Church put them to, and thus identify its context or life-setting (*Sitz-im-Leben*) and sift out the original teaching from the later additions, is known as *form criticism*.

In the 60s AD about thirty to thirty-five years after Jesus' death, a man known to us as Mark decided to write down some of the stories and sayings of Jesus. He did not intend to collect all the material he could find in order to preserve it for ever; in fact, he was quite selective. His Gospel is short, only fourteen chapters long, and as the evangelist John would later say, 'There were many other things that Jesus did; if all were written down, the world itself, I suppose, would not hold all the books that would have to be written' (Jn 21:25). Mark's purpose was not to write a biography of Jesus. He deals only with a brief span of Jesus' life, his public ministry. Mark knew that Jesus' ministry began at his baptism by John and ended with his death. That was the ancient kerygma, the early Church's proclamation of faith (Acts 10:37-38). But within those fixed points he did not know the order of events or their original setting. What was available to him was a number of stories and sayings, used in different situations in his own Church. From these he devised an entirely new literary form, the Gospel, moulding his material in order to proclaim his message: 'The Good News of Jesus Christ, the Son of God' (Mk 1:1). This opening verse serves as both a title and a declaration of intent.

Mark takes the reader on a journey with Jesus through his growing isolation, rejected by the leaders of the people (3:6), by his kinsfolk (3:21) and townsfolk (6:4; 6:6), misunderstood by his own disciples (8:33; 8:34-35; 10:35-41), to his cry of abandonment on the cross: 'My God, my God, why have you deserted me?' (15:34). Throughout the ministry Jesus' identity is cloaked by commands to silence (1:24; 1:34; 1:44; 5:42). It is only at his death that any mortal being recognises Jesus as who he really is: the centurion declares, 'Truly this man was the Son of God' (15:39). And the veil of the temple is torn from top to bottom, the barrier separating the realm of God from the realm of mankind is broken down and Jesus' purpose has been achieved.

Perhaps Mark was writing for a persecuted Church. Certainly he wishes to show the cost of being a disciple — the cross, and the reward — truly knowing Jesus. The true disciple for Mark is the blind man, Bartimeus (10:46-52). He is the one who really 'sees', and seeing, 'he followed Jesus on the road', the road to Jerusalem and the cross.

Mark had an insight into the mystery of the person and work of Jesus that he wished to proclaim and he selected and moulded his material to reveal his insight.

In the 70s AD Matthew and Luke wrote their Gospels for their communities. The Gospel of John reached its final form in the late 90s AD. Again none of them had the intention or the means of writing a biography of Jesus. Rather each has his own insight into the mystery of Jesus and his own genius for expressing this truth, working with the material that has come down to him in the tradition.

Matthew, for instance, writes for a predominantly Jewish community, and part of his purpose is to show that Jesus is the new Moses who gives a new Law from the mountain. Luke writes a two-volume work in which he shows Jesus to be the Lord of history, standing between the age of the Old Covenant and the new age of the Church in the Spirit. John more than any of the Gospels brings the divinity of Jesus into focus.

The study of the creative role of the evangelist (*redactor*) and his particular theological and Christological insights in known as *Redaction criticism*. This work is helped by tracing the ancestry of the texts to see how the evangelist has changed and adapted the material that has come down to him. Close scrutiny of the texts convinces most scholars that both Matthew and Luke used a version of Mark's Gospel as well as material common to them both, and material unique to each. John, however, bears little similarity to the other three Gospels. This examination of the relationships between the Gospels and the history of the texts before they were brought together by the evangelist is known as *source or literary criticism*.

It is clearly not possible to construct a 'Life of Jesus' from the Gospel accounts. However, rather as an archaeologist scrapes through layers of remains of past cultures to even more ancient relics, so scholarship can filter the Gospel texts, indicating the hand of the evangelist, the life-setting in the early Church, to reveal with some certainty words which Jesus himself spoke, actions which he himself performed. Thus few would doubt that Jesus performed wonders — healings and exorcisms; or that the parables are 'a fragment of the original rock of tradition' (J. Jeremias, *The Parables of Jesus*, SCM Press, 1954).

But we must not imagine that only the actual words and acts of Jesus can lay claim to being the truth. All levels of development in the history of the tradition of the Gospels and of the Bible are inspired by the Holy Spirit and give witness to the involvement of God with his people. Though the question of truth requires a more nuanced answer then at first appears, nevertheless we can strongly affirm that the Bible is true, profoundly true. **"**

Attitudes to Scripture

The second reason the question, 'Why Scripture?' is important is that it makes us look seriously at how we use the Bible in practice. It is unfortunately the case that very often Scripture is misused and mishandled. What we believes the Bible is *for* effects the way we operate with it. If we believe it is primarily provided to give us a literal answer to every present-day situation then we shall use it differently from someone who believes it is primarily a means God uses to reveal himself. If we believe it is *only* for private, individual spirituality which has no contact with how we live our lives then we shall use it differently from someone who believes it has a challenge for our social and corporate life as well. So, we need to think through the question, 'Why Scripture?' if we are not to engage in an unbalanced use of the Bible.

We need to look carefully at the methods we use and see whether they are suitable both to our own situation and to a balanced approach. Some practical questions here may help when we come to try to assess methods:

- Is the method relevant to our situation (i.e. is it scratching where people itch)?
- Is life as we know it and the Scripture method related?
- Does the method encourage people to discover for themselves or does it give all the answers?
- Is the method too academic? Is it stretching enough?
- Does the method seem to encourage people to read too much into the text?
- Does the method help people in their spirituality without neglecting the consequences for living the Christian life?

Attitudes to God

Finally the question, 'Why Scripture?' is important because it forces us to look carefully at our attitudes towards God. What sort of God does the Bible show him to be? What do his actions tell us about him? Does he communicate with us now?

Most of us would say that we believe God is active and wants his children to come to know him. But if he does communicate with us the question is, how? How do we know what he is like? God's dealings with us are, of course, far too numerous to be mentioned. If we have eyes to see and ears to to hear we discover him in all sorts of situations. We discover him through the world he creates, through the people around us, through our contact with others and through our experience of the Church, both local and universal. However, it is also true that the Bible shows us what sort of God we are engaged with. It is through Scripture that we have the record of his dealings with his children, his leading of his people in the Old Testament. It is through the Gospels that we have our pictures of Jesus, the Word made flesh. It is through the Acts of the Apostles and the letters that we see the infant Church growing in its understanding of God's will. If we fail to allow ourselves to be exposed to this richness we are missing out on a basic way of discovering God. Such failure means we have not listened to the words of St Jerome: 'Ignorance of Scripture is ignorance of Christ'.

The process of discovering what God is like and what he wishes to communicate to us is what all the methods in this book are designed to encourage. It is the purpose of all Bible work.

■ How is Scripture to be interpreted?

One of the real difficulties with using Scripture is that there is no such thing as a neutral reading. Every single person interprets the Bible according to his or her background, life experiences, culture and tradition. Some people read the Bible from below, some read it from above. Unless great care is taken the text can be manipulated. Without necessarily being conscious of what they are doing people can read into the Bible their own feelings and thoughts. The interpretation can be based more on what they think than on what the Bible actually intends to say. The result is distortion. The message of the text does not get through. We end up speaking to the Bible rather than letting it speak to us.

For this reason the Church has always stressed that we must be very careful about how we interpret the Scriptures. The Bible does not stand in total isolation from the tradition, history and teaching of the Church; it is part of that tradition. It is the root of the teaching of the Church and that teaching cannot be ignored in our interpretation of what we read. Most readers of this book will be part of a particular Church tradition. It shapes us and makes us what we are today. We cannot pretend that background does not exist. That tradition is important because it helps us feel we belong, it gives us our identity and it provides us with the stories of previous generations from which we can learn. Our generation will make its own contribution.

So tradition is not something static; it is part of a process in which we are all involved.

Now, because the past makes us what we are and because it contributes immense riches from which we can learn, our work with Scripture must take this into account. If our interpretation of Scripture is in line with the faith experience of past generations and in line with what countless Christians have discovered to be true we shall not be in danger of false intepretation.

■ Why Scripture in the Parish?

Although in many of our parishes the Bible has received new emphasis it is still true that too often it is either misunderstood or simply not thought about. The attitude can be rather like a comment I heard last year. One of the local shops at Christmas had made a display in the window which depicted a Christmas scene complete with manger, star and all the trimmings. In the forefront was a Bible open at Luke's account of the Nativity. It was while looking at this that I overheard two people talking. 'Look at that,' said one, 'they are even dragging the Bible into religion now.' Sometimes one gets the feeling that a similar thought runs through the minds of many Catholics! Why all this emphasis on the Bible all of a sudden? Such an attitude will not be altered unless the Bible becomes real and meaningful, and this can only happen if it is seen to be important throughout the whole of our parish life. Scripture should not be relegated to the liturgy, nor even to small Bible groups. Rather, sharing God's Word together should be a natural part of our common journey in faith and a normal part of our Christian experience, both alone and with others. There are three important points to be made here.

1. *This basic Scriptural approach to parish life is not as 'way out' or as difficult to achieve as it may seem at first sight.* The problem arises if we see the Bible as something only within the grasp of the educated few and only relevant to certain areas of our common life. In fact, working with Scripture and through Scripture can be a surprisingly 'natural' activity. The Bible is, after all, The Book of prayer and a manual for Christian life.

What I am really pleading for here is that we see the Word of God as holistic: that is, that through it the parish is able to hear God speaking in *all* its activities, that it is able to grow towards that vision of God's people which the Scriptures speak of, and that it finds in them guidance, nourishment and above all the living presence of God.

2. *Part of that holistic approach to Scripture must be its place in ministry, using that word in its widest sense.* That lay people are now more involved in the life, worship and mission of their local church and are now encouraged to fulfil an active role is one of the fruits of Vatican II. Gone are the days when the only task of the lay person was to 'pray, pay and obey'! However, the concept of 'many ministries' is not always easy to accept or to implement. Sometimes it has been difficult for the clergy to encourage the laity to see themselves as having a true ministry to fulfil. Sometimes it has been difficult for the laity to persuade the clergy to let go of some of the

essentially non-priestly functions. (For a fuller treatment of this idea see Monica Comerford and Christine Dodd, *Many Ministries*, CTS, 1981.) Where it has happened there are still difficulties. Leaders of groups, readers, catechists and lay pastoral visitors all need help and guidance in the important ministries they now seek to undertake.

I believe that a true Biblical spirituality can be the basis for the real development, both of individuals in the exercise of their vocation and of the community they seek to serve. A dialogue with God in Scripture can do this because:

- it can provide a treasury of prayer and spirituality for the exercise of many ministries in the parish;
- an encounter with God through Scripture can enable such people to discover their own vocation more fully;
- Biblical sharing with others can give much needed affirmation to them as they carry out their tasks;
- a scriptural grounding can provide them with a wealth of riches in their dealings with others.

3. *The Bible is the Book all Christian denominations have in common.* The Church has always held that the Scriptures are one way of obtaining nourishment for the journey of faith. As *Dei Verbum* says, the Church has always venerated the Scriptures

> 'as she venerates the Body of the Lord, since from the table of both the Word
> of God and the Body of Christ she unceasingly receives and offers to the faithful
> the Bread of Life.' (*Dei Verbum*, 21)

We cannot deny that in the past in the Roman Catholic Church this view of the importance of Scripture for ordinary people has sometimes been overlooked. Fortunately, in our day there has been a real resurgence of interest in the Bible. Catholics, along with other Christians, are now encouraged to read and digest the Word and to see themselves as people of the Book. This resurgence of interest in the Scriptures has brought to the fore an awareness by many Catholics that there is a lot we need to learn from others whose experience of the Scriptures is so rich. One of the great movements of the present ecumenical situation is that many inter-church groups have developed with the express purpose of Bible Sharing or Study. Our common Book is giving us an opportunity to come and share together.

■ How can we get started?

The practical aspect of how to get going with Scripture will be dealt with in the rest of this book, but it is worthwhile making some very general comments here. These are, as it were, basic ground rules.

Firstly, if we wish Scripture to play a more central role in the life of our parishes we should always have before us some basic aims. We must:

- aim at ensuring that Scripture is a natural and integral part of our life and not a forced 'extra';

- aim at ensuring that our plans are concerned with allowing God to speak through his Word as a means of dialogue with his people;

- aim at ensuring that our plans are concerned to help not only individual growth but community growth as well;

- aim at ensuring that all use of Scripture is relevant to every group or individual who uses it. This entails a sensible and sensitive selection of Scripture. Do not choose a passage from Leviticus for use with a Mother and Toddler group!

- aim at ensuring that Scripture is accessible to all people, academic or not, clever or not, literate or not, and that it is accessible to all groups of whatever kind;

- aim at ensuring that our plans are concerned with helping people not just to acquire exegetical knowledge but also to develop communication skills;

- aim at ensuring that our plans never contain Scripture merely as a 'back up' for doctrine;

- aim at ensuring that our plans concern God's Word through Scripture to the world beyond our doors.

Secondly, we need to be clear that there is a distinction between Bible Study and Bible Sharing. One of the real difficulties of helping people step over the threshold into the Bible is the fear that it is too difficult. Many small groups soon begin to flounder because they are trying to run before they can walk. This is especially true if there is no one in the group who has a background in Biblical studies. Unfortunately, many people assume that to enter the world of the Bible and discover its message for today requires a considerable amount of Biblical scholarship. Many groups are encouraged through discovering other ways of arriving at a contemporary application of the text.

Therefore it may be helpful to make a distinction between Bible Study and Bible Sharing. Both of these are important. Bible Study — that is, discovering the message of the text for those to whom it was originally addressed — is vital. Through it we are enabled to see God's dealings with his people then and its implications for today. Bible Sharing is a way of enabling people, whether they are articulate or not, academic or not, young or old to discover the Word of God for themselves. Both Bible Study and Bible Sharing should be integrated. On the one hand we must recognise that not everyone can start with in-depth Bible Study, whereas everyone can make a start with Bible Sharing. On the other hand, Bible Sharing must be aware of the importance of Bible Study. Groups using Bible Sharing methods should take into account the riches of Biblical scholarship. This book will mainly be concerned with Bible Sharing methods which can help us liberate the Word of God from the shackles in which it has been placed. It assumes, however, that continued growth in faith through the Scriptures requires awareness of the insights of Biblical scholarship. The ideal is that Bible Sharing and Bible Study should complement each other. All work with the Bible, whether as an individual or in small or large groups, needs to look at both what the text meant for the original hearers and what it means for us today. Our understanding of the latter can be incomparably enhanced by discovering the former.

SMALL GROUPS AND SCRIPTURE

IT WAS A TUESDAY NIGHT and the youth group were due to meet, as they did each Tuesday, at the local school where they hired the tennis courts for the evening. Most were not church-goers at all — simply keen on tennis or friends of the small nucleus of church-goers. This Tuesday was important. The autumn was drawing on and there was a need to discuss what the group was to do during the coming months, tennis being out of the question.

'We thought we might do something quite different,' said Mark, a fifteen-year-old member of our church choir. When I asked what sort of thing, one or two suggested perhaps a chance to talk 'about things that mattered', as they put it. I suggested they go away, think about 'what mattered' and meet at my flat the next week. To be honest, I didn't expect much, so I was somewhat surprised (to say the least) when about a dozen turned up and, sitting crammed in my study supping coffee, they decided they would look at the Scriptures. Together during the winter we looked carefully at Jesus as the Scriptures portrayed him — a new experience to many, and a real eye-opener to all. For a good number this was their first experience of handling Scripture, and for some the first time the person of Christ became a real and living force. It will always be a joy for me to remember Margaret's exclamation as for the first time she read Mark's account of Jesus' denunciation of the Scribes and Pharisees. 'This Jesus,' she said, 'sure didn't beat about the bush,' and I shall long remember the look of enlightenment on her face as she said it.

For many, be they young people or adults, contact with the Bible in any real sense comes within a small group. That group may be especially formed with the intention of doing something Biblical, or it may happen that Scripture naturally forms part of the agenda of a group whose primary purpose is different. Either way, learning from each other and sharing with each other is of primary importance. This happens best in a small group where people can get to know and trust one another. There can be no doubt that this is one of the chief ways in which a real and meaningful encounter with God through his Word can take place. As far as Scripture is concerned, groups in the parish bring both rewards and difficulties. In this chapter we shall look at some of the different types of groups, at how to set up a group, and some guidelines for leading a group.

_____ SECTION 1 _____

Types of Groups

'Can you come and speak to our Bible Group?' is a request I frequently receive, and I frequently ask, 'What sort of Bible Group do you have?' Often the question seems to meet with surprise because many people assume that Bible Study is much of a muchness and one group must be much like another in what it does and how it functions. Nothing could be further from the truth. Apart from the fact that no two groups are ever alike, simply because no two people are ever alike, there are different types of groups and different ways of handling Scripture within a group. The most common method is usually called Bible Study and it often runs into difficulty. The reasons vary but usually the problem centres around the need for someone in the group who knows something about Biblical scholarship. As some people put it, 'We need someone to tell us what this means'. Nevertheless, these Bible Study Groups are very important and so we shall begin our consideration of how the Bible can be used in small groups with a look at the aims, methods, joys and frustrations of this type of group.

■ Bible Study Groups

The basic aim of a Bible Study Group is to understand the text. What did the author intend to say to those to whom the message was first delivered? What sort of text is it? How does it fit in with the context? What difficulties does it raise for us today? This method really requires someone who can act as a resource person, who has enough knowledge or access to knowledge to explain the text. It requires a leader who, if not very conversant with Biblical scholarship, can at least be confident in handling the difficulties and knowing what and what not to look for in a commentary on the text.

Studying the Scripture in this way is vitally important because it ensures that people do not end up distorting the text. It is unfortunately true that the Bible can be made to say practically anything if verses are taken out of context, or if passages are not read with some awareness of the situation to which the authors were addressing their words.

Bible Study, therefore anchors the text and helps us to see it in context. It helps to prevent us from reading into the text. Bible study, then, focuses on the text and asks what it meant to the original hearers. Only then do we ask the question, 'In the light of this background what meaning does it have for us?'

The method usually consists of:

● reading the text;
● studying the text with the help of commentaries, cassettes or a 'resource person';
● considering the question, 'What does this mean for us?'

Here is one such example. It is one of a series of sessions used by a group working their way through the Book of Amos.

EXAMPLE

Step 1   Opening prayer by a group member. Before reading the text we let ourselves relax and remember God's presence with us.

Step 2   One member reads the passage slowly (Amos 5:21-24):

I hate, I despise your feast,
  and I take no delight in your solemn assemblies.

Even though you offer me your burnt offerings and cereal offerings,
  I will not accept them, and the peace offerings of your fatted beasts
  I will not look upon.

> Take away from me the noises of your songs;
>   to the melody of your harps I will not listen.
>
> But let justice run down like waters,
>   and righteousness like an ever-flowing stream.

Step 3   Allow a short time for silent reflection.

Step 4   The leader gives a commentary on the passage, using a number of resource books and discovering the major theme. In this passage the dominant theme was seen to be that God, through Amos, was condemning Israel's form of worship. The people were putting worship in place of social responsibility and were engaging in worship which had no connection with the world of injustice around them. Amos castigates not the worship itself but what the people had made of that worship. It is unacceptable to God because the people of Israel do not live as the people of God. As such they are at odds with him. A renewal of righteousness is necessary so that worship can once more be what God wants.

Step 5   Work through the questions. There is no need to cover them all. Work at your own pace.

1 What do you think would have been the reaction of those who heard these words of Amos? Why?
2 Underline the pronouns in the passage. What does this show about the relationship between the people and God as Amos sees it?

3 What do you think is the overall evaluation Amos gives of Israel's worship?

4 What do you think it means to 'let justice roll down like waters and righteousness like an ever-flowing stream'? What are our present-day injustices in our own community? What are we doing about them?

5 Can you see any similarities between the situation Amos addressed and our own situation today? Is our worship linked to our concern for social justice?

What to watch out for

1. The principal problem with the Bible Study method is that it needs a leader or teacher with enough knowledge to handle the text adequately. Failing this, there must be someone with enough experience to know how to use commentaries well, and it is not always possible for a group to have access to someone like this. Frustration and disillusionment can set in if members of the group feel that they are struggling without any such help.

2 Bible Study undertaken in this way can easily become divorced from real life. Sessions can be good and useful intellectual exercises in discovering the text but have little relevance to the real lives of those in the group. This is one of the reasons why some groups using this method fail to attract new members and often cease altogether after a comparatively short period.

3 Relying on academic research alone may lead to utter frustration and, above all, may alienate many people who feel they are not clever enough to take part in such an exercise. The result is that some groups end up knowing a lot about the Scriptures – indeed, they may know a lot *about* God, but they fail to know God himself as a living reality.

Despite these problems it must be stressed that these Bible Study groups are very valuable. They enable people to tackle the text together and to explore its meaning, which they may not have been able to do alone. Such groups also ensure that there is no 'private reading' of the text. It is very easy to make the Bible say what we want it to say. Reading the passage in its context and with an awareness of its meaning for the original hearers enables a group to approach the text with open minds. It stops us from reading into the text meanings that are not there! However, these Bible Study groups are not the only way of using the Scriptures in a small group. There are ways and means of exploring the passage which do not need to have an 'expert' present and which focus on the meaning of the text for the here and now in the light of the author's original intention.

■ Bible Sharing Groups

Unlike Bible Study, which aims to understand the Word in its context and then to ask its meaning for us, Bible Sharing groups aim primarily to discover the meaning of the text for today. The focus is less on the original meaning of the text and more on its meaning for each group member personally. Therefore there is less need in these groups for an 'expert'. However, such groups do need a good facilitator who is able to draw out from the members what the passage says *to them*.

Bible Sharing groups are much more varied in the way they operate than Bible Study groups. They are more flexible and can be adapted so that the Scriptures can be used relevantly in a variety of situations. Groups can be large or small, and the method can be used by parish organisations, families, youth or special-interest groups. If small groups are set up *specifically* to do Bible Sharing, there are three main methods such a group might follow. Firstly, the group may decide that it wishes to share a passage together as a means of praying the Scriptures. Secondly, the group may decide to take a theme from everyday life and explore what the Word of God has to say about it. Thirdly, the group may wish to take a passage from Scripture and see what it has to say about their own situation. Following is an explanation and example of each of these three methods of Bible Sharing.

Method 1: Praying the Bible

Prayer groups are common in many parishes. Such groups, set up primarily with the purpose of providing a setting for shared prayer, can be extremely difficult to sustain in any meaningful way. There are a number of reasons for this. Firstly, such groups can become very 'clique-ish' – they can seem to be the prerogative of a chosen few. Those who attend may be well aware of this and wish with all their hearts that things were different. However, this is how it appears to many outside the group. Secondly, prayer groups run the continual risk of becoming very inward-looking. Even if the members see their function in mainly intercessory terms there is often a division between prayer and activity. Often such intercessory prayer may be either too parochial – in the worst sense of the word – or too far-ranging, so that the participants feel a gulf between their prayer and their daily activity. The third difficulty concerns variety within such a group. After a while there is a real problem because there is no focus which will feed the intercessory prayer to which the members feel called. Lack of a focus for thought and meditation can mean that groups 'get into a rut' in which the same petitions are mentioned meeting after meeting, and in which everyone begins to know what everyone else is about to say. Finally, prayer groups can become excessively vocal, leaving God no room to speak. The use of Scripture in such a group can help in all these areas. It can provide a focus through which the group members can listen to the Word of God as well as talk. It can be a guard against lack of variety and it can, if used well, help to bridge the gap between prayer, meditation and everyday life.

In a prayer group Scripture needs to be handled especially sensitively. The primary purpose for the group is to enable Scripture to become a vehicle for prayer, both spoken and unspoken. Using a chosen text for shared prayer can be done in a number of ways. Here are two examples showing how Scripture can be used in a prayer group.

EXAMPLE 1   ## LOOK UPON MY SON

Step 1   The group begins with a time of silent prayer and quiet reflection.

Step 2   One member reads the passage slowly (Luke 9:37-43):

> On the next day, when they had come down from the mountain, a crowd met him. And behold, a man from the crowd cried, 'Teacher, I beg you, look upon my son, for he is my only child; and behold, a spirit seizes him, and he suddenly cries out; and it convulses him till he foams and it shatters him and will hardly leave him. And I begged your disciples to cast it out, but they could not.' Jesus answered, 'O faithless and perverse generation, how long am I to be with you and bear with you? Bring your son here.' While he was coming the demon tore him and convulsed him. But Jesus rebuked the unclean spirit and healed the boy, and gave him back to his father. And all were astonished at the majesty of God.

Step 3   Read the text again for yourself. Pick out one phrase or word which stands out for you (e.g. I beg you; look).

Step 4   Each person reads out their phrase or word. NO discussion yet.

Step 5   We share *why* we chose the phrase or word. Others should listen carefully and only when all who wish to do so have contributed should discussion be allowed.

Step 6   We pray together in the light of the passage, both for others and for ourselves.

The second example comes from the Fellowship of Contemplative Prayer. This method is especially suitable for those who find extempore prayer rather difficult and who would prefer a more contemplative approach. The text used here is from Isaiah 43:1. In this method it is best to use very short texts which can be easily remembered and in which God speaks to his people directly (i.e. in the first person). Scripture abounds in such sayings both in the Old and New Testaments. For instance, from the New Testament one could use some of the great 'I am' sayings of Jesus. The leader should encourage people to repeat the text in their own minds during the periods of silence, especially if they find their thoughts are wandering.

What is given here is taken from the booklet *Towards contemplation* by Peter Dodson (Fairacres Publications, 1977), but those who wish to explore this method further would do well to get in touch with the Fellowship. Peter Dodson describes the method as follows:

EXAMPLE 2   ## I HAVE CALLED YOU BY YOUR NAME

"I would like you, the reader, to imagine that you are a member of a group of, say, a dozen people. You have come together for an hour or so. I am with you, and my job is to introduce you and the rest of the group to an experience of contemplative prayer.

First we sit up straight and still. An upright chair will help us do this . . . we breathe in deeply. As we sit quietly we allow God to call us into his rest, using words like those from St Matthew 11:28 and Psalm 46:10. 'Come to me, all whose work is hard: whose load is heavy and I will give you rest . . . Be still and know that I am God . . . Come to me . . . Be still . . . and rest . . . come . . . rest . . . rest . . . come . . . rest.

(Silence for about two minutes)

Now we bring to *mind* the particular words we have selected for this contemplative prayer exercise. Let the words come to life in our minds . . . I do not mean that we have to spend our time struggling to *understand* the words. Our task is simply to take them in and let them live, just as we might soak up the music of a great symphony. 'I have called you . . . you are mine . . . YOU are mine.'

(Silence for about five minutes)

In our first period of silence we have received the Word of God as far as we were able into the mind. The Word is becoming part of the way we think . . . And now, as far as possible, take the Word of God to *heart* . . . Let the Word dwell in you richly . . . let the words of the text become part of the rhythm of our breathing and our life. 'I have called you . . . you are mine . . . you are *mine*.'

(Silence for about five minutes)

Now we are ready to give our time and attention, as far as we are able, to other people and the world. Using our *imagination* to the full, we can begin by picturing members of our own individual family group . . . if you do not have a family in quite this sense picture instead those closest to you: relatives or friends. Take care and time over this. Contemplate them . . . look at each in turn and, as far as we are able, share God's desire and longing for them . . . In our own minds and hearts we speak the Word of God which is becoming part of our word. 'I have called you by your name, you are mine.'

(*Short silence*)

And now we broaden our vision to include the Church family of which we are a member. 'I have called you . . . you are *mine*.'

(*Short silence*)

And so we could go on using that God-given gift of imagination, achieving a vision of his concern for the life of our nation, the world and the whole of creation. 'I have called you by your name . . . You are mine . . . you are mine.'

(*Short slience*)

Closing prayer by the leader.

That concludes the contemplative prayer exercise. At first the group leader would be well advised to stick to the fairly rigid exercise outline of the kind we have shared. But once the group has begun to grow in mutual trust, the third section of the exercise can take on a much freer expression of concern for the well-being of others. *All* the group members may be invited to raise subjects for prayer . . . the leader always ending with a repetition of the main saying."

Method 2: Our lives reflected in the Bible

The second method of Bible Sharing starts with a consideration of our own lives and then turns to the Scriptures for reflection. This method has the advantage of starting from a consideration of real life and, if used sensibly, can open the eyes of many people to an awareness of how relevant the Biblical message can be. The general structure of this method is simple:

● It starts with a present-day situation (this may be a consideration of some local issue or it may be something taken from the newspapers or magazines).

● After a period of discussion about the topic the group then turns to a Biblical passage to see what light the Scriptures throw on the situation. This passage must be carefully chosen beforehand.

● The group considers whether any action is necessary in the light of its discoveries.

EXAMPLE   THE GOD OF SUFFERING

Step 1   We begin our meeting with a short period of quiet. One member of the group opens with a short prayer asking the Lord to direct our minds and hearts.

Step 2   The following article is read:

When the gas cloud descended so suddenly on the city of Bhopal in India many of the inhabitants were asleep. One of the first rescue workers on the scene said, 'India is no stranger to tragedy but somehow this one was different. It would somehow not have seemed quite so bad if it had been workers alone who were injured but so many of the victims were children – just children asleep. It was terrible to see them, terrible. My head tells me it was a man-made disaster, the fault of our own scientific advancement but my heart cries out, the children, oh God, why didn't you spare the children?'

Step 3   Share together your honest feelings about the passage and about tragedies such as Bhopal or famine or earthquakes. Share your own experiences of suffering which seems to be senseless.

Step 4   One member reads this passage (Matthew 27:38-48):

The two robbers were crucified with him, one on the right and one on the left. And those who passed by derided him, wagging their heads and saying, 'You who would destroy the temple and build it in three days, save yourself! If you are the Son of God come down from the cross.' So also the chief priests with the scribes and elders, mocked him, saying, 'He saved others, he cannot save himself. He is the king of Israel; let him come down now from the cross, and we will believe in him. He trusts in God, let God deliver him now, if he desires him; for he said "I am the Son of God" . ' And the robbers who were crucified with him also reviled him in the same way.

Now from the sixth hour there was darkness over the whole land until the ninth hour. And about the ninth hour Jesus cried with a loud voice, 'Eli, Eli, lama sabacthani?' that is, 'My God, why hast thou forsaken me?'

Step 5   Share together what you think the story of the crucifixion says about God and suffering. Share some of your own experiences of having known, or not known, the presence of God in your own times of suffering, whether physical, emotional or spiritual.

Step 6   How does our discussion help us in our contact with any people we know who have to cope with suffering?

Step 7   We pray together, thanking God for the death and resurrection of Christ, for all who serve and relieve those in distress and for all those who need our prayers in their sufferings, that may be aware of the presence of Christ.

This second method has the great advantage of starting where people really are. Although almost any present-day situation could be handled in this way it is not always easy to choose a correct text. The leader (or someone else in the group) must have enough knowledge of the Scriptures to pick out an appropriate text, which really does relate to the situation and is not in any way twisted or forced to make it fit in with the theme.

Method 3: From the Scriptures to our own situation

This third method consists of starting with the Bible and then looking at our own situation to see what light the Word of God can shed on it. In other words, the method starts with the Bible and works towards our own lives. This way of using Scripture normally has the following pattern:

- the passage is read;
- we ask what situation in our lives the passage is addressing;
- we reflect on what the Word is saying to our situation;
- we ask what effect our discussion should have on the way we live our lives.

EXAMPLE

THE CALL OF GOD

Step 1   The meeting opens with a short time of prayer.

Step 2   A member of the group reads the passage (1 Samuel 3:1-10):

> Now the boy Samuel was ministering to the Lord under Eli. And the word of the Lord was rare in those days; there was no frequent vision.
>
> At that time, Eli, whose eyesight had begun to grow dim, so that he could not see, was lying down in his own place; the lamp of God had not yet gone out, and Samuel was lying down within the Temple of the Lord, where the Ark of God was. Then the Lord called, 'Samuel! Samuel!' and he said, 'Here I am!' and ran to Eli and said, 'Here I am, for you called me.' But he said, 'I did not call, lie down again.' So he went and lay down. And the Lord called again, 'Samuel!' And Samuel arose and went to Eli, and said, 'Here I am, for you called me.' But he said, 'I did not call, my son; lie down again.' Now Samuel did not yet know the Lord, and the word of the Lord had not yet been revealed to him. And the Lord called Samuel again the third time. And he arose and went to Eli, and said, 'Here I am, for you called me.' Then Eli perceived that the Lord was calling the boy. Therefore Eli said to Samuel, 'Go, lie down; and if he calls you, you shall say, "Speak Lord, for thy servant hears".' So Samuel went and lay down in his place.
>
> And the Lord came and stood forth, calling as at other times, 'Samuel! Samuel!' And Samuel said, 'Speak, Lord, for thy servant hears.'

Step 3   The group discusses the text. What does the passage say about God? What does it say about ourselves?

Step 4   What sort of situations in our own lives are linked up with the passage? When have we heard God calling us? In what situations? In what way does he call?

Step 5   Are there any situations in our own personal lives where God is calling us to act or think differently?
Are there any situations in our community where God is calling us to act differently?

What to watch out for

These Bible Sharing methods are probably easier for many groups to use than Bible Study. However, certain potential problems must be noted.

1. The major problem with the Bible Sharing methods is to ensure that the Scripture is used properly and that the text is not misused. In the second method (Our lives reflected in the Bible) there is a danger of twisting the text so that it fits the situation under discussion. In other words, of hunting for a text to suit our topic – or even worse, of trying to make a text say what it was never meant to say.

2. In the third method (From the Scriptures to our own situation) the leader must be able to ensure that the group really hears what the passage itself is saying and is able correctly to identify a situation to which it relates.

3. A third difficulty arises from the fact that there are some areas or problems which the Bible does not deal with directly. Leaders must be aware of this and resist the temptation to make the Scriptures say everything for every situation.

_____ SECTION 2 _____

How to set up a small group

Some small groups working with the Bible form themselves quite naturally. A few people with a common aim and desire get together and make their own arrangements. However, sometimes the parish may wish to set up small groups for a specific purpose. It may be for Lent or for Advent. If such is the case it is best to bear the following points in mind.

Getting people together

It is usually best to invite people personally to join a group. Often the response will be more positive to a personal invitation from a friend or neighbour than if a general appeal to go along to a group is made. However, if the parish is used to meeting in small groups it is possible to put up lists of the venues and leaders at the back of church and encourage people to sign up for one of these. If these groups can meet on different days and at different times it enables people to have a wider choice. They can then attend the group most convenient for them. A balance of both of these methods, personal invitation and general appeal, is ideal because it increases the number of new people who might only come if personally invited and yet gives freedom of choice to others.

Size

Make sure you plan the right size for the group. Too large a group inhibits free discussion and makes sharing more difficult. Six to ten is the ideal number. The group will not function well once you get above this. If you have more than ten or at the most twelve, you may need to split the group. There are two ways of doing this. The group can be divided in half, OR if the group is quite big it can 'bud'. A leader with just a few can form themselves into the nucleus of a new group and draw in new members. However this splitting is done it is usually painful. People are naturally reluctant to break up and leave old established patterns for new ones.

What venue?

Make sure that you have the right venue for your group. By and large, most small groups will meet in a home. Sometimes a group might meet in a church hall or some other neutral venue. There is something to be said for both these venues. Naturally, meeting in someone's home is much more informal and the atmosphere is usually more conducive. People feel able to relax and be themselves sitting in a comfortable room among their friends. However, there are some people who are shy of joining a group and going along to another person's home. I had an example of this in a parish where groups never seemed to work until we discovered that the reason was very simple. The parish was comprised of a large council-owned housing estate and a large privately-owned area of housing which was occupied largely by professional people. Most groups were held in the homes of these people. Only when a group started in the parish hall did we draw in those from the other side of the parish. As one of them put it, 'We feel more at home here. We could never have fitted in down there.' Sometimes people need a neutral venue in which to meet, at least to begin with.

However, the problem with meeting in a place like a church hall is that it can be very soul-destroying. There are not many parish rooms which give the warm, friendly atmosphere which small Bible groups require. Often such rooms are full of the remains of last month's jumble sale and the equipment used by the pre-school play group is piled up around the walls! If this is the case there is no need to abandon hope.

Atmosphere

Having the right atmosphere is vitally important, whether the group is meeting in a home or in a neutral venue. People must be helped to feel relaxed and at home. It is also important that the atmosphere for our sharing or study of the Scriptures is a prayerful one. Creating this atmosphere in which people can grow and develop is not difficult.

Make sure the lighting is right. It is best not to have a glaring fluorescent strip. Try a few table lamps about the room instead. Obviously it has to be bright enough to allow people to see what they are doing but it should not be intrusive.

Make sure you have some sort of focal point. This may be something like an open Bible and vase of flowers on a small table, or a lighted candle. It could be a picture or an object related to the theme of that session. There are endless possibilities, given a little imagination.

Make sure you use music occasionally. Background music can set the scene, or perhaps sometimes the group could engage in some singing. Sometimes, reading the Scripture with quiet music in the background can aid concentration.

Make sure people are seated comfortably. Chairs should normally be in a circle. It is very important that everyone can see everyone else and that no one is seated outside the circle. If you are meeting in a very large room or hall make sure the group meets in a corner with the chairs arranged in a circle so that a more intimate atmosphere is built up.

Make sure everyone can hear well.

Aim

Make sure you know *why* your group is meeting. Always have a definite aim in mind. Are you going to engage in Bible Study, in Bible Sharing or are you a particular-interest group who want to use the Scriptures as a way of reflecting on your particular work within the parish or community?

How often?

Decide in advance how frequently you are going to meet. Almost all small groups function best if they operate on a termly basis with holidays in between. People are far more likely to come if they know that they are committing themselves for a specific length of time. Very often groups which meet week in and week out eventually die, not because people are no longer interested but because the need for breaks and holidays is not catered for. People then become unwilling to join for fear they are committing themselves once and for all.

The periods of Lent and Advent are ideal for meeting, as they give a focal point. Groups that are 'on-going' would probably do well to consider meeting for, say, six sessions. In some areas it may be best if groups meet every fortnight rather than every week. This allows people to have more flexibility with their diaries and to make a point of attending every session without doing damage to their other important commitments.

Keeping the channels open

Make sure the group or groups do not become an 'in thing'. In other words, avoid any sense of clique. It is very important that the *whole* parish is informed of what is going on and is kept in the picture regarding the findings of the groups. This can be done through the parish bulletin, through handouts, or through the magazine. It can also be a help to have talks or 'open evenings' on what has been happening. If you have more than one group it is essential that the groups meet together and share what they have been doing and discovering. This could be done once a 'term'.

✱   ✱   ✱

Leading a small group does not mean that you have to be an expert in the subject under discussion. However, there are techniques which can help leaders, many of them very simple and straightforward ideas which can enable a small group to function better. It is to this task of leadership that we must now turn.

SECTION 3

Leading a small group

Working in small groups can be notoriously difficult. People often act very differently when they are in a group. It is important to understand how a group functions, some of the difficulties which may arise, and the best way of leading a session. In this section we shall look at the task of the leader, types of leadership and the leader's role. In every group people behave in different ways so this section will also look at phases of a group and the various ways in which people learn within a group setting. I am grateful to the Church Army for permission to adapt ideas and materials from their leaflet *Small Group Leadership* in what follows.

The task of the leader

Leading a small study group can be a daunting task. This is especially true for those who have not done so before and who feel uncertain about how to proceed. The purpose of a small group is to provide a setting where growth and learning can occur. Consequently, the best results are usually obtained from leaders who give plenty of scope for discovery and personal initiative. So you will no doubt be glad to hear that you do not have to be an expert! In fact, research has shown that groups have greater difficulty getting people totally involved if an 'expert' is present. Nor will you have to supply all the answers. The main task is to supply the framework which gives the needed security for people to think and speak. The success or failure of a house group depends almost entirely on the leader, so your role is vitally important.

Types of leadership

We have made the general point that the leader is there to 'facilitate' the group. It must be added that different groups need different kinds of leadership at different times. These different styles of leadership will produce different reactions in the group and these can be shown in diagrammatic form.

1. The Talk
Here the speaker gives out and members take in.

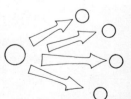

2. The Expert-led Discussion

Here the interaction is between the leader and various individuals.

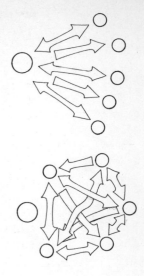

3. Discussion

Here everyone is involved, not just with the leader but with the other members of the group. Everyone will have something to contribute in different ways. Some will want to do most of the talking, others will be content to remain silent.

Most parish study groups need to aim at a balance between 2 and 3 above. New groups may need to start with 1 and move on to 2 or 3 as time progresses and a sense of openness increases.

Different types of behaviour

The group leader will soon notice that in a group people behave in different ways at different times. At any one time the leader may notice the following are present:

The Dominant – will quickly assert his or her prescence. Able to put thoughts into words, he or she may be the sort others look to for guidance. Not necessarily uncooperative or aggressive, this person may still try to make a 'takeover bid' for the group.

The Talkative – may be nervous and may talk to cover this up. Whatever the reason, care must be taken to ensure that he or she does not monopolise the group.

The Silent – must be handled with great care. There may be a very good reason for remaining silent, perhaps embarrassment or a feeling of inadequacy. The leader needs to be very sensitive as some people do need to be allowed to remain silent. Others can be drawn out by asking a direct but simple question. Never, never make the person feel pressurised.

The Deviant – delights in being different. Comments from this person may well help to break the ice and produce a bit of humour. Unorthodox comments may also help others to think more clearly for themselves. However, he or she can be a sort of 'demolition contractor' who, with one sentence, can shatter the progress of the group.

Always remember that as much time should be spent getting to know the members of the group as getting to know the study material.

Group learning

The leader must have eyes open to understand what is happening in the group at any given moment. People should be:

- valued and accepted for themselves;
- able to discover that their gifts are useful and wanted;
- free to discover themselves in the company of the rest of the group;
- able to make discoveries for themselves and have the support of the rest of the group in that discovery.

Evidence shows that people usually learn best in a group. It gives them the chance to ask questions, to grow at their own pace and sort things out for themselves. However, there are a number of things which hinder effective learning in a group. It is important that the leader is aware of these and is able to spot them when they occur:

- Effective learning nearly always ceases if we stop listening. This can happen for a number of reasons. Firstly, it can happen when I think I know what the other person is going to say. Secondly, it occurs if I am very anxious to speak myself, and thirdly, it can happen if my emotions are running high so that I do not concentrate on what the other person is really saying.

- Effective learning nearly always ceases when the speaker uses long words or phrases which I do not understand. I switch off if I cannot grasp what is being said. The use of religious language, therefore, needs to be carefully watched.

- Effective learning ceases when an argument develops in which both parties are determined to have the last word.

- Effective learning ceases when two or more people try to speak at once. Sometimes a private conversation develops between two people in the group. The leader must make quite sure that only one person is speaking at a time, however heated the discussion might be.

Arising out of this it is important to remember that, even if I am leading a group, people will still not listen if I ramble on, speak for too long, am aggressive or exaggerate. It is important to look at people. (However hard you may find it, do try to make eye contact with people in the group.)

The role of the leader

Here are some practical hints about actually leading the group:

Before the Meeting
- *Know your material.* If you are going to use ready-made discussion starters or notes, they will almost certainly need adapting to your particular situation.

- Make sure the practical arrangements are sorted out. Are you having tea or coffee at the beginning or the end? Is the seating right? Can people see and hear adequately?

At the Meeting

- Greet people as they arrive.

- Try to make sure everyone knows everyone else. (You may have to do introductions for a few sessions if you are starting a new group.)

- If the group is new it will amost certainly expect you to do most of the talking. This may be necessary at first, but do not let the group pressurise you into its own mould. Take the opportunity early on to explain what you, as leader, are trying to do.

- Keep the group on the track. Try to distinguish between genuine questions and red herrings! Some side tracks will need to be investigated even if they lead nowhere.

- Interpret and explain. Unclear contributions from members must be sorted out.

- Protect those who are under attack. There will be personality clashes in most groups. Differences of opinion should be brought out into the open but without developing into an out-and-out argument.

- Be sensitive. Powerful emotions are sometimes let loose in a group. Try to imagine how others are feeling, especially when they feel threatened. People who are finding some of their long-held beliefs under question may well react very strongly and aggressively. They may also need to 'take it out on someone' – probably you!

- Make sure the group never 'gangs up' on one individual. Even if you suspect that this is likely to happen, call a halt. Take care not to jump on people who you feel are making irrelevant or silly comments. Try to lead them gently back to the main theme. Never ignore them altogether.

- Summarise the discussion at appropriate points and *always* stop on time. The group can always go on unofficially if it wishes, but people must be given the opportunity to leave without feeling embarrassed.

- Liaise with other groups where necessary. Discuss the future with the group itself if you feel that all is not going well.

After the Meeting

- Do not worry about what has happened!
- Plan well for your next meeting in good time.

★   ★   ★

Conclusion

This chapter has covered a good deal of ground. Small groups are undoubtedly one of the most valuable means for growth and development. In them people are able to discuss and share their own experiences in the light of the Scriptures. However, even in small groups great flexibility is needed when it comes to our method of handling the Scriptures. Even the two general methods outlined above, Bible Study and Bible Sharing, must be open to a wide variety of both themes and techniques. One of the real difficulties we have had in the past regarding the use of the Bible is that we have not been adventurous enough in the way we handle it. We have not used enough variety, nor have we taken into account the different ways in which people learn. In other words, we have not been creative enough, and it is to this subject of variety and creativity in our handling of Scriptures that we must now turn.

THE CREATIVE USE OF SCRIPTURE

I N THE LAST CHAPTER we looked at how Scripture can be used in small groups especially set up for the purpose of studying and sharing the Biblical message. It is unfortunate that this is often seen as the *only* way to explore Scripture within the parish. The tendency has thus been to push Scripture to the sidelines for 'those who like that sort of thing' and it has not always become that life-giving force which can enrich and enhance other areas of our life as a community.

If the Word of God is to take its rightful place in our lives it is vital that we widen our view of how and when to use it. We need a much broader approach than we often have at present. There are two words in particular which are of the utmost importance in helping us to allow Scripture to be that living Word of God in our communities as a whole. Those two words are *Variety* and *Creativity*.

The need for variety

The need for variety in the way we handle the sacred text is of vital importance. It is necessary for two reasons in particular. Firstly, we need variety because everyone, regardless of their intellectual ability or skill at putting thoughts into words, has the *right* of access to God's World. We are not all good at articulating but Scripture is for everyone. It is for those who are good at thinking things out logically and for those who are not, for those who are literate and those who are not, for the young as well as the old. Variety in the way we present the text is vital if we are not to discriminate about who can and who cannot engage in this encounter with the message the Bible has to offer.

Secondly, we are all at different stages on our journey of faith, so variety in presenting the text is necessary if we are not to fall into the trap of thinking that only those who have gone a certain way along the Christian path can be involved in this encounter with Scripture. We all have different intellectual, psychological and emotional needs, and we are all in need of hearing the Word of God wherever we are on our journey. People will hear this message in different ways. Because we are not all the same, and because we are all at different stages and have different talents, some of us will hear it through discussions but others will discover its meaning through the use of their eyes. Others will relate more if they are able to explore their everyday situations and experiences in the light of Scriptures and others if they can express their reflections on the text through art or music or drama. So, if we are not to alienate some people we must use many methods to enable them to discover for themselves what God is saying to them through the Scriptures.

The need for creativity

The second key to a good and meaningful use of Scripture throughout the parish is creativity. Too often we have been over-cerebral or over-intellectual where the Bible is concerned. We have not opened up the text in a creative way for people, and the result of that, instilled into the minds of many, is the belief that Scripture is only for those who can cope with abstract intellectual thought or those who can master the niceties of Biblical criticism. As we have seen, the intellectual, thoughtful approach to the Bible is vital if we are not to go off into flights of fancy and make the text say whatever we want it to say, but we must also recognise that a little more creativity in the way we handle the text might open up the Scriptures to a wider group.

Creativity and variety in the way we handle the text are, therefore, essential. The use of many methods and techniques can bring us to the point where the Bible takes on a new meaning for us. Indeed, it is sometimes only through the use of the non-verbal or non-cerebral processes that we come to grasp what God is really saying to us through his Word.

★　　★　　★

This chapter gives a number of examples showing how Scripture can be used in a variety of creative methods. Hopefully they will give a 'taste' of how wide and deep the use of Scripture can be; that they will show that the Bible message can reach out to all people, whatever their situation and ability with words; and finally that they will illustrate that Scripture can be used in a variety of situations within the parish community. Each method will be preceded by a short explanation and comment about its value and how it might be used in the parish. Most methods shown can be used in either small or larger groups (which can be sub-divided if necessary). Other examples and further ideas for methods of using the Bible can be found in Chapter 8.

SECTION 1

Using our eyes

It has to be admitted that for a vast number of people the visual is of far more importance than the written word. Many, if not most of us, are used to receiving the information we require through our eyes. We now hear and see the news through our televisions without having to rely on newspapers which need to be read. We have a wealth of good educational programmes which both inform and entertain us. Receiving information visually and acting on it is now part of our everyday life. For example, the widespread acceptance of the necessity for wildlife conservation among ordinary people is in no small measure due to the splendid natural history programmes we see on our televisions. In school, too, the emphasis, quite rightly, is not *only* on books but also on discovery for oneself in other ways.

Whatever judgements we make about this use of the visual and its importance in our present world it is, nevertheless, a fact that many people now obtain the information they require through visual means, with very little reading involved, and they make judgements accordingly.

Given this situation it is hardly surprising that some individuals should feel very uncomfortable when faced with a written text (either from the Bible or from some sort of written material to go with it). The situation becomes acute if the page is one of blank text, printed in small type, sometimes in two columns, and unenlivened by any visual matter. What the page *contains* may well be within the individual's abilities to grasp, but the *presentation* may well be wrong for his or her situation. The result is that many people are 'put off' before they start.

The creative use of visual material, which need not be expensive or elaborate – indeed, it can be homegrown – can bring a passage to life.

Here is an example of how one group took a passage from St Luke's Gospel and altered it for a visually-oriented group. The original material consisted of the text followed by some fairly academic and intellectual questions printed underneath on one side of A4 paper. Here is what the group did with it.

Choosing pictures

EXAMPLE

WHO DO YOU SAY I AM?

Step 1 The group spent a while talking over what had happened to them since they last met. This period is extremely important. It allows people time to exchange news and to relax.

Step 2 There was a period of quiet and a short opening prayer led by the group leader.

Step 3 The leader placed on the floor about twelve or fifteen pictures of Jesus. These were taken from prints from old masters, stills from films, modern art, and popular 'home pictures'. Each picture had a number.

Participants were asked to note the number of the picture they felt spoke to them.

Step 4 Luke 9:18-20 was read by a group member and time for reflection allowed.

Step 5 Participants were encouraged to tell why they chose the picture and what that picture told them about who Jesus was for them. This was done without discussion.

Step 6 Finally, the group discussed what their collective picture of Jesus was like: what relevance did it have for their lives today?

Step 7 The group meeting ended with prayer.

Describing a poster

There are other ways of using the visual element within Bible Sharing. One very effective way is to take a picture or a poster which expresses a present-day situation and to use it as a way into the Scriptures. In this example the picture used was a black-and-white photograph of a broken jug. The picture showed only the shattered glass jug in close-up. The group was considering the whole theme of forgiveness and reconciliation.

EXAMPLE   ## OUR BROKEN LIVES

Step 1   The group discussed together what had happened to them during the last week. In particular, they were asked to share any experiences of failure or brokenness. How did they feel? What effect did it have on them?

Step 2   The leader opened with a short prayer.

Step 3   The group wrote down on a large sheet of paper how they felt about their experiences of being broken. This was done without discussion or comment from other people. Words such as hard, angry, painful, guilt were written on the sheet without comment.

Step 4   The group then looked at the poster of the broken jug in silence for a few moments.

Step 5   Members discussed together what they saw in the picture. Comments ranged from 'It can be mended' to 'It can never be the same again'.

Step 6   The group next turned to the Scriptures, and in particular to the gospels, to find examples of the broken people who came into contact with Jesus. Two or three examples were chosen (Zacchaeus, Mary Magdalene). The passages were read and the group discussed:

- in what ways were these people broken;
- how did they feel;
- in what ways did Jesus heal their brokenness?

Step 7   Finally, the group discussed what these passages had to say about their own broken lives and God's action within them.

The meeting closed with a short prayer.

Creating a picture

One other very simple (and very cheap!) method of using the visual is to allow people to make their own visual material in the course of their discussion. When I first tried this method I was a little concerned that people might be embarrassed about drawing in public but, in fact, I soon discovered that if it is done in twos or threes people soon lose their inhibitions, especially if the leader makes a point of insisting that we are not interested in artistic ability! The great advantage of this method is that it enables people to put down on paper what they might otherwise be unable to express in words. Its other big advantage is that it can be great fun, and there is no reason why understanding, sharing and discovering the Scriptures should not be a thoroughly enjoyable experience. Here is one example of the principle in action.

EXAMPLE   ## DRAWING OUR LIVES

Step 1   People shared together what had happened to them during the last week.

Step 2   The leader opened with a short prayer.

Step 3   The group was split into threes. Each small group was given a large sheet of paper and some felt pens and asked to draw their parish church community (as they saw it now, not as they would like it to be in the future).

Step 4   The pictures were displayed and people given a chance to look at one anothers'.

Step 5   The group discussed together what their pictures said about their local community.

Step 6   One member read 1 Cor 12:4-31. A few moments of silence were kept so that people could re-read the passage after it had been read aloud.

Step 7   In the same group of threes people were asked to draw how they would like their parish community to be, bearing in mind the reading from 1 Corinthians. (They were encouraged to draw some other design rather than the body mentioned in the Scriptures.)

Step 8   These pictures were also displayed and a chance given for people to look at one anothers' work. The group then reassembled and discussed together what their drawings said about the sort of Christian community they felt they would like to see develop in their own local area.

The group closed with a prayer for the guidance of the Spirit on the work and mission and life of the parish.

_____ SECTION 2 _____

Using our ears

We have already seen the importance of the visual in using Scripture creatively. Of equal importance is the use of our ears. People learn through listening. They learn through listening to each other, they learn through listening to music or to plays, readings or to poetry.

The advent of good (and small) audio equipment has opened up for us a whole new range of possibilities as far as Bible Sharing or Study is concerned. They are part of our modern way of life, and it is important that we use them in our proclamation of God's love through his Word. In this section are a number of examples intended to give an indication of the scope and variety of audio aids which can be used in our discovery of Scripture. None requires particularly complicated equipment and all can be done by a parish group or groups.

■ CASSETTE STUDY AIDS

There are on the market a whole range of cassettes which can be used by small groups in their study of Scripture. As with most things the content and standard is very variable. Unless you have heard the tapes before, buying these study aids can be a risky business. However, it may help to point out some dos and don'ts concerning buying and using this material.

Dos

1 Try if you can to buy tapes which have been recommended to you by others. It is always dangerous to buy on the off-chance that it will be good.

2 Try to buy tapes which are in short and manageable sections. It is extremely difficult for a group to listen to a disembodied voice for longer than about eight to ten minutes. Many of these cassettes will give a talk for anything up to 45 minutes. If you are buying such a tape make sure that you listen to it carefully well before the group meeting. You can then carefully divide the tape up into short manageable sections, stopping every ten minutes or so to allow people a chance for discussion.

3 Make sure that everyone can hear the tape clearly, that it is neither too quiet nor too loud. Do try to buy tapes which have material for group use included with them, such as leaflets or questions. If possible try to ensure that every group member has a copy of this.

Don'ts

1 Don't overdo the use of cassette tapes in a group. To have session after session of this method can be very draining.

2 Don't rely solely on the cassette tape. If you are using a cassette in a Bible Study Group make sure that you also have other resource material to which you can refer should the need arise. Don't try to cover too much at one time.

Provided that they are used with sensitivity and care, ready-made cassette study aids can be a very useful means of enabling us to share more fully in the Word of God.

■ HOME-MADE CASSETTES

There are all sorts of possibilities for a group to engage in an encounter with Scripture through making its own recording of the implications the passage has for group members. There are all sorts of ways of doing this. Perhaps the best way is to decide on a passage from Scripture which can be easily dramatised and which has a good story line. The group could simply record the passage using a number of voices; it could engage in simulated interviews; it could include musical items, discussions or news comments.

The rest of this section suggests ways for a group to explore Scripture through this medium.

Taping the Gospel

EXAMPLE ## LAZARUS COMES TO LIFE

The Raising of Lazarus (John 11:1-44)

The group decided to explore the implications of this passage by using a series of interviews. They required one person to play the part of Martha, one for Mary, one for Lazarus, a couple of onlookers and one narrator or interviewer.

The group first read the passage carefully, slowly and prayerfully. Group members tried to immerse themselves in the scene and to enter into the character they were to play. The interviewer began the tape as if it were a news item. 'I am speaking to you from Bethany, a small village outside Jerusalem, where a remarkable event has just taken place . . .' The interviewer then spoke to each of the main characters, trying to draw out from them firstly what had happened, secondly their reactions, and thirdly what difference it was making to them and their future.

This process will probably take two or even three group sessions if it is to be done well. The group needs time to discuss carefully this passage before the interviewing actually takes place.

There are other ways of doing the recording. For instance, this same passage could be used as a piece of straight reporting with one or maybe two people telling the story in modern, everyday language. Alternatively, it could be undertaken as a magazine-style recording: that is, it could be a combination of interviews, perhaps with a musical item in the middle; discussion, as if it were a studio panel talking about the implications of this event; and some researched background given by a 'special correspondent'. This multi-style approach can add to the work-load as it requires more research, but it can also be great fun.

When the recording has been made there are a number of possibilities for its use. Naturally the major reason for making the recording was to enable the group to discover more about the passage for themselves. However, there is no reason why such a cassette could not be used or shared with a wider audience. It could, for instance, be used by another group, or as a focus for a school assembly. If the group has been really imaginative they may even find that the local radio may be interested.

A final word of warning needs to be given about engaging in this method. It is vitally important not to let people read into the text. The leader should always keep a very close eye on the passage and ensure that the group is not superimposing things that are not there.

Recording interviews

One final way of using a cassette within Bible Sharing or Bible Study is to encourage people to interview others on specific subjects. When the interviews have been played the group listens carefully to what people have to say, and then turns to the Scriptures in order to discover God's Word for that situation. Here is how one group made use of this technique.

EXAMPLE

The parish had been thinking a good deal about how to reach out to people on a large housing estate in the parish. A small number of people from the estate already came to the church, and together with other Christians in the area the houswives had been visited door-to-door. This had uncovered a number of families in difficulties of one sort or another. Now some people in the parish wanted to set about some sort of active community building on the estate. Others in the church were uncertain about this and wondered whether this sort of activity was really the job of the parish. The parish decided to explore both their own situation and what Scripture had to say by undertaking the following exercise.

A number of questions were asked of different people in the area and their answers recorded with a portable cassette recorder. These questions were asked of:

- people on the estate who were not churchgoers at all;
- members of the congregation who lived on the estate;
- members of the congregation who did not live on the estate.

In all cases an attempt was made to ensure that a good cross-section of ages and sexes was contacted. The same questions were asked of all.
These were:

- What do you think are the major problems of people living on the estate?
- Do you feel there is any sense of community?
- Do you think the local church should be involved?
- If not, why not? If so, in what way?

From all the tapes a 'master tape' was made giving a good selection of the answers. This tape, along with a written analysis of all the answers, was considered at a parish meeting. This meeting had three main sections:

- a reading from the Letter of James 2:14-23, followed by a period of silence and prayer;
- the tape was played twice (it only lasted about 8 minutes);
- a consideration of what people were saying (this included a look at the written analysis);
- a re-reading of the passage from James, after which the large group was split into smaller units to consider what God seemed to be calling the community to do in the light of both Scripture and their present-day situation.

This exercise could, of course, have been carried out without the cassette recordings. However, the advantage of recording interviews with people proved to be twofold. Firstly, people did not have time to work out logically what to say — so what emerged was 'gut' reaction. Secondly, it enabled a very accurate analysis to be made in that there was no chance that the interviewer could alter or distort the views of those interviewed. This can easily and unwittingly happen if the interviewer has to write down the answer.

Using music

The use of music can, like a certain brand of lager, reach the parts that others cannot reach! There are a number of ways of incorporating this into Bible Sharing work.

1 Music can be used very successfully to create the right atmosphere. As we shall see later, atmosphere is very important: the setting and the feel of the situation needs to be right and can help greatly in allowing us to be open to hearing God's Word.

2 Music can be used as a background to the reading of Scripture. This background music, sensitively chosen and used while the Word of God is read, can sometimes bring out new insights from the passage.

3 Music can be used directly as the means of opening up a specific subject. This music may be either specifically religious or secular. For instance, there are many good popular songs whose lyrics can be used either to get discussions started or to summarise our discoveries.

EXAMPLE

LONELINESS

Step 1   The group leader begins with an opening prayer.

Step 2   The group listen together to the song *Eleanor Rigby* by the Beatles. A moment of silence is kept.

Step 3   The group discuss:

- What does this song say about loneliness?
- How true is the song?
- Who are the lonely people?
- Why are they lonely?
- What does loneliness do to people?
- What can be done about it?

Step 4   The group then turn to the Scriptures. Mark 14:32-42 (the Gethsemane story) is read slowly and prayerfully.

Step 5   The group discuss:
- Was Jesus lonely?
- What did he experience?
- How did he feel about the sleeping disciples?
- What does the passage have to say about coping with loneliness today?

Step 6   The group listen again to the song *Eleanor Rigby*.

Step 7   The group have a short period of intercessory prayer for the lonely people of the parish.

Using poetry

Poetry like music, can 'reach the parts that others cannot reach', and can be used as a way of entering more fully into Scripture. A great deal of Scripture is poetic in any case, but it is good for a group sometimes to use secular poems as a means of exploring similar themes within Scripture. A great deal of poetry is specifically religious, or at least has religious overtones, but much that is not overtly religious can also be used. One way of using poetry is to encourage people to bring along their favourite piece, whether religious or not. Participants can be asked to read out their poem and to share about why it appeals to them. What does it say to them? What message is it conveying to them? Often it will be possible to see within the Scriptures similar attitudes and similar pieces of poetic work expressing a similar theme. This will be especially true of the Psalms. Undoubtedly some people will bring along with them poems of great joy and happiness; others may bring along with them poems containing thoughts of sadness or depression; yet others may simply bring along poems because of the words and the musical quality which they contain. All these themes, joy and happiness, sorrow and depression, can be found within the Psalter.

It may be possible for a group actually to form and develop its own Liturgy of the Word with the use of poems. For instance, I have seen the Stations of the Cross very beautifully expressed through the use of a combination of secular poems and Scripture readings. At each Station there was a reading from the Bible and a reading from a secular poem expressing the theme of that Station. This combination of poetry and Scripture can be extremely powerful.

SECTION 3

Using the written word

One of the problems in handling a text of Scripture is that it can sometimes be over familiar to us. We know the story backwards. We think we know its meaning. We fail to see in it new or different meanings because we are blinded by our own familiarity. One way of overcoming this problem is the use of simple techniques which will enable us to see the text afresh. These techniques can, of course, be used with a text which is unfamiliar to us. Here are three examples of how to use very simple methods for discovering, or rediscovering, what the text is actually saying. These methods and techniques can be used in a fairly large group as well as a small house group. People can share in twos and threes what they have discovered and written down. Here are the three methods in use. A passage from St John's Gospel (1:35ff) was chosen, the same passage in each case.

Underlining

Having decided on a passage, ask people to underline recurring words or phrases, or ask them to underline all the verbs in the passage, or ask them to underline all the contrasts in the passage, then discuss.

EXAMPLE

Step 1   A time of quiet reflection by the reading of the passage. This is done prayerfully, and a good period of silence is allowed after the passage has been read so that people may re-read it by themselves.

Step 2   People are asked to underline what the various characters in the passage were doing (e.g. John was *standing*; the two disciples *heard* him; Jesus *turned*; etc).
- What impression do you get from this passage about what people are doing? (The group should be able to suggest from their underlining that there is a great deal of movement in this passage.)
- What movement occurs in the passage from the beginning to the end?
- What does our underlining tell us about how we should follow Jesus?

Brainstorming

Read the passage and ask members to say in one word what they think the main point of the passage is. List these on a large sheet of paper. When everyone has contributed, look for the signs of similarity and the signs of difference as to what the passage is saying.

EXAMPLE

Step 1   As in the previous example the passage is read slowly and prayerfully and time is allowed for people to reread it.

Step 2   On a large sheet of paper the leader or the scribe writes down the immediate reaction of group members to the question, 'To see and meet Jesus means . . ..?'. Members should call out the answers that immediately occur to them, in one or two words. No discussion is allowed by other group members until the list is complete.

Step 3   The group then discusses what coming and seeing Jesus means for us.

Using sentences

Take a passage and, having read it slowly and prayerfully, ask each person to complete individually a sentence such as, 'To me this passage says', or, 'For me the major theme of this passage is', or, if the theme is quite clear, a sentence such as, ' . . . (theme) to me is . . .'.

EXAMPLE

Step 1   As in the previous two examples the passage is read prayerfully and time is given for reflection.

Step 2   Each individual is given a sheet of paper on which is written the sentence, 'To me finding the Messiah means . . .'. Some time is allowed for people to write down their answer individually.

Step 3   The answers are shared in groups of three, or possibly in pairs. (Allow about ten minutes for this.)

Step 4   The whole group comes together and brainstorms about what finding the Messiah means for that community.

SECTION 4

Using drama

The Bible is a living Book. It is full of dramatic action. Within its pages we have examples of the way many people expressed God's message, not only through words but through actions. The use of very simple drama can help us enter deeply into the text, to become part of it and be immersed in it. It allows us to participate, to watch the story unfold, and it allows us to see and hear what is set before us.

To use drama does not necessarily mean that we have to put on a performance. It can be used in big groups or in small and people do not have to be good actors. Above all drama can be fun. With a little imagination and the minimum amount of props a group can be very deeply involved in a passage of Scripture.

Role play

Like drama, role plays can enable people to enter the text at a level other than thought alone. No acting is required here but there are a few golden rules that should be borne in mind if role plays are to be used:

1 Try to ensure that people are given roles very different from their actual situation.
2 Never pressurise anyone into taking part if they would rather not.
3 Keep as close as possible to the text.
4 Always allow plenty of time after the exercise has finished, in order to discuss what has happened.
5 Ensure that people are 'de-rôled' before the sessions finishes; make sure that people do not take their rôle away with them.

Here is one example of using a passage of Scripture as a very simple role play.

EXAMPLE ## THE ELDER BROTHER

About 25 or 30 people are needed to undertake this successfully.

Step 1   Arrange the seating as follows:
There should be three groups of chairs, one group to the left of the leader (about ten people), one group to his or her right (about ten people) and about five in front of the leader.

Step 2   Give all three groups their role. The group to the left are the upright citizens of the town, probably biased towards the establishment and conservative by nature. They are God-fearing, religious people who, by and large, have made their way in the world.

The group to the leader's right are the 'tavern' people out for a good time, whose motto is, 'Live today for tomorrow we die'. They can see little sense in building for the future and prefer to spend money when available and enjoy what they can.

Immediately in front of the leader sits the family, whose youngest son leaves home with his share of the inheritance.

Step 3   Ask participants to open their Bibles at the story of the Prodigal Son (Luke 15:11-32). When all have found the place, have someone read it aloud.

Step 4   Allow a short time for people to re-read the passage.

Step 5   The leader goes through the passage, verse by verse, picking out the main thrust of the story and stopping to ask each of the groups how they felt about what was happening. So, for instance, the leader may begin by asking how the family felt when the younger son came and asked for his share of the property. What did the upright people of the town think about this? Did the 'tavern' people think the lad had done wisely? The leader should continue with this questioning throughout the story, asking the groups for their reactions and drawing out from them what their thoughts are about the action of the story as it progresses. Were the tavern people glad to see the newcomer or did they just want his money; did they care about him when famine hit the land? How did the upright people feel when the son came home? Did they think the father had let him off too easily? How did the family feel about the son's return? What did the elder brother think about it all? What did the rest of the family feel about his refusal to go into the party?

This activity will probably take a considerable amount of time to complete.

Step 6   The leader should finish by asking each group the question, 'Did the elder brother go into the feast or not?'

This method of using the text is particularly valuable because it allows it to speak for itself. It avoids the danger of reading into the parable later Christian interpretations and allows the story to stand on its own merits. It allows the story to do what Jesus intended it to do in the first place, that is, to challenge us and our own attitudes.

Chapter 4

PARISH ACTIVITIES AND SCRIPTURE

IN THIS CHAPTER we shall look at the way Scripture can be used within a whole range of parish activities: not special events or initiatives specifically undertaken to study Scripture, but the ordinary events which go on in our churches week after week and year after year. We shall look at the place of the Bible in liturgy, in adult education, in preparation for the sacraments, in pastoral care and in evangelisation. As in the other chapters examples will be given of how parishes have successfully used Scripture in these areas of their life.

SECTION 1

Scripture in the Liturgy

It is a cold winter's morning. The congregation have battled through the bitter wind. Mrs Robinson slumps into her seat with relief after struggling with the problem of getting her three children up, breakfasted and ready in time. She wonders whether Andrew, her husband, will manage to get their usual parking space. In the row behind, Mr Williams is worried because he had real trouble getting the car started this morning and he has a horrible feeling that it could be an expensive job. Next to him, Gillian Rudge is feeling somewhat jaded, having flown back from a business trip to Berlin late last night. Eileen Field envies her. She is tied to her home for seven days a week; six floors up with a mentally handicapped child to care for and a husband she has not seen for months.

Each member of the congregation comes with their own set of hopes and fears, joys and sorrows. Some will be distracted during worship by what is going on in their own lives. Others will be distracted by what is going on in church. John finds it difficult to concentrate because the youngest Robinson child keeps turning round and beaming at him. He can't help but smile back. Joe can't keep his eyes off the monstrosity of a hat that the woman in front of him is wearing.

Into this situation the Word of God is proclaimed. Not all are attentive and ready. All have preconceptions of what is happening during the reading of the Scriptures. Some will already have switched off, automatically assuming that it will have little to say to them. Others believe in theory that God speaks through his Word but are distracted. Some may consciously tune in to hear what is being read.

For many this listening to the reading of Scripture in church will be the only time in the whole week that the words of the Bible will be heard or read. What relevance does it have for them? What do they make of it? How can this proclamation be more effective and meaningful for them?

The use of the Bible in liturgy, therefore, requires an awareness of the situations in which most of the listeners will hear the Word. It also requires very careful and prayerful preparation.

■ THE PLACE OF THE LITURGY GROUP

In many Roman Catholic parishes (and not a few Anglican ones) liturgy groups have been formed. These vary greatly in what they do but the general idea is that all those involved in the Sunday (and weekday) worship meet together on a regular basis. They discuss and plan the liturgy, going through the readings, picking the hymns, considering the prayers, etc.

Advantages

● *Support*. Liturgy groups offer support to those engaged in the Sunday worship. Any sensitive priest or minister knows the difficulty of trying to plan the liturgy. If the worship is fairly well-structured and normally follows a definite path, as in the Roman Catholic tradition, then the difficulty is trying to keep it fresh so that it is more than something people 'go through' every week. If the worship is more flexible the difficulty is trying to give it enough structure so that people know where they are and have some idea of the elements that will be present. Liturgy groups can offer support to those planning worship and they can offer a cross-fertilisation of ideas which one person alone cannot hope to achieve. Of course, there are those responsible for leading worship who would feel very threatened by such an idea. Unfortunately a good number of these may not also realise that the Sunday worship they lead has lost its life-giving quality for many in the pews.

● *Cohesion*. The second function a good liturgy group can perform is to give cohesion to the worship. If readers, those leading the prayers, musicians, the president and any others taking part 'get their act together', the whole liturgy is more likely to be centred around a theme and hang together. There is nothing worse than a service at which the readings are pointing out one theme, the preacher ignores it, the prayers are not linked to anything and the hymns are picked because they happen to be the organist's favourites! What a liturgy group can offer is the chance for the Word of God, the prayers, hymns and sermon to be seen to be part of one act of worship. In other words it can help worship to become holistic.

● *Planning*. The third area in which a liturgy group can be used is in the planning of special services. This may be for the major Christian festivals such as Christmas or Easter; it may be harvest festival, penitential services or some community act of worship (such as civic services). Here the group can take a particular theme and plan the worship around it, possibly including drama or special music or poetry, in fact whatever seems to speak to that situation. Together the group can sort out the readings and ensure that the Word of God is applicable to the celebration.

How such groups fulfil their aims varies greatly from place to place. Some meet weekly, some monthly. Most include in their meetings a study of the Word which is to be proclaimed. By going through the readings the group not only prepares for worship but itself engages in a living encounter with the Scriptures.

Potential problems

It would be wrong to suggest that all is sweetness and light with liturgy groups.

Difficulties arise from a number of sources.

● There are problems if some of the key people are not present at the meetings. It is vital that the priest or minister or leader of the worship is present. If this does not happen things are likely to fall apart.

● The key person, or persons, must refrain from being seen by the rest of the group as the 'expert'. Preparation should be truly shared by all, including the priest or minister who must resist the temptation to tell the group what he or she wants. The preacher should not tell the group what the subject of the sermon will be and then expect the group simply to produce the 'back-up' material. For many this real sharing which involves give and take is not easy.

● The group must never be seen as a clique by the rest of the parish. Keeping the channels of communication open with the community and allowing new people to join are essential.

■ THE PLACE OF THE READER

In most churches the reading of the Scriptures has an important place in the liturgy. In the Roman Catholic Church in particular the place of the proclamation of the Word has been highlighted in recent years. This has meant that for many the Scriptures are being given a new importance. In many churches the actual reading of the Word is undertaken by a variety of people, some better than others at this vital task of communicating the message. The way in which the Scriptures are read – that is, the actual practical business of reading out loud – is unfortunately often taken for granted and little help is given to those involved. There is a real art to reading well and many simple but effective techniques can be learnt. These can enable the hearers better to understand God's message.

The task of the reader is not easy. He or she often has to battle with several difficulties. Firstly, there may be the physical difficulty of the building itself. Bad acoustics, poor amplification systems or awkward 'dead spots' can all cause problems. Secondly, there may be distractions of one sort or another inside or outside the building. The Council have decided to repair the pavement and reverberations from the pneumatic drill are echoing around. A child falls off the pew and yells in pain. Such distractions are inevitable and so it is necessary to be prepared for them as far as possible. Thirdly, and perhaps most difficult, the reader has to cope with proclaiming a passage originally written in a different culture and for different circumstances. The message may be eternal but the world of ancient Israel is not the same as ours. Nor is the Church at Corinth in exactly the same position as our church. The reader has to take into account that people are inclined to switch off when the talk is about the Perizzites and the Hittites! So the reader's task is to proclaim the message of the passage intelligently so that people can be helped to relate to it. Fourthly, there is the problem of what might be called reverential insensibility. We have heard the passage before, reverently we listen to it and we think we already know its message in all its fullness. Somehow that very familiarity can prevent us from really hearing the Word. The reader, therefore, has to make the passage live and to help us to hear it as if for the first time. How, then, can a reader help the Scriptures come alive for the hearers?

Preparation

It is essential that readers prepare well for their task. To proclaim the Word well requires that it is understood by the proclaimer. That means making sense of the text not only intellectually but personally. The text must speak to the reader. In other words, in order to be read well the passage must be assimilated by and live for the person whose task it is to proclaim it. Both the understanding of what the passage is about and a personal response to it are necessary. That means looking at the text in at least three ways:

- looking at the text itself;
- looking at the text in its original setting;
- looking at the text for today.

The following illustrates one way in which readers can get into the text using this pattern. It can be used individually or in a group.

EXAMPLE

1. The text itself

Step 1   Read the text carefully and slowly.

Jot down what impresses you, raises questions for you, confuses you.

Step 2   Now read the text again and mark:
- words that keep recurring;
- words that contrast;
- words that correspond.

Who is involved in the action?

What do they do or say?

What tenses are the verbs?

Step 3   Now try to see what is actually going on in the text.

Does anything happen between the beginning and the end?

Who is doing what or seeking what?

2. The text in its time

Step 1   Put the text in its setting.

How does it fit in with what comes before and after? (You may need a commentary to help with this.)

Step 2   What was the situation of the people?

Can you think of any other passages like this elsewhere in the Bible?

If the passage is from the New Testament does it pick up Old Testament themes?

What sort of writing is it? Is it poetry or law or teaching or prophetic oracle or what?

Why do you think this passage was recorded? What question or problem does it set out to answer?

3. The text for today

Step 1   Now reread the text and ask:

Who am I like?

What does this say about my life?

What does this say about my relationship with God?

What does this say about my community?

Step 2   Try rewriting the text so that it speaks to you now.

Take your time over the whole exercise. Do not hurry the process.

Proclamation

The next area to be considered is the actual proclamation itself. Here some very practical points need to be made.

● The reader should feel at home at the lectern. Be familair with the layout of the Lectionary or Bible and ensure that it is open at the right place before the service begins.

● The reader should remember that it is his or her task, not just to communicate a bundle of words but to communicate an experience. The reader must become an interpreter for the congregation as well as communicator of the actual words of the passage. That means that there needs to be contact between the reader and the congregation. This is done not only with the voice but also with the eyes. Readers should *look* at the people. Eye contact is very important, so the reader should aim to speak the last phrase of each sentence looking at the congregation.

● The words of the passage should be thought of not as individuals but in bunches. The listeners need to hear parcels of sound. So the reader should ask: what is the tone of this passage? Is it rebuking, commanding, persuading, praising, condemning? How are the words phrased? It is this phrasing which is the essential difference between the written and the spoken word. It enables the reader to emphasise the words that are important to the sense and allows time for the congregation to take in what is being said.

● If an amplification system is used it is important to check that it is switched on and working before the service – not immediately before the reading. There is little worse than a microphone being hit with the fingers just before the reader begins. If the microphone is not working then project your voice accordingly.

● Read slowly but vary the pace. Boredom is usually caused by monotony. The reader will therefore need to vary both speed and the tone of voice during the passage.

● Sanctimonious voices distract! It is important that precious speech is avoided. Read clearly but without shouting – remember, there is a difference between projecting the voice and shouting. Remember too that a microphone will carry the voice but it will not amplify it.

● Sentences should not be allowed to 'trail off'. Make sure the voice does not drop at the end of a phrase or sentence. Words should be finished off in the same way. However, beware of reduplicating consonants at the end of words or allowing words to run into one another (e.g. Noah's Sark!).

● The reader should try to ensure that he or she does not 'fiddle' at the lectern. Sliding hands up and down the book or even nervously jangling keys in the pocket can happen unconsciously but can be very distracting. Try not to move about too much or the focus will be on the reader and not on the reading.

● If it is the custom to end the reading with a phrase such as 'This is the Word of the Lord', a good pause should be allowed between the reading and the ending. The phrase should then be said with conviction.

● Movements to and from the lectern should be made confidently. Readers should look as if they are meant to be going there and not sneaking up on the rails! Take time. Proper movements and reverences add to dignity and a sense that the proclamation of the Word is important.

● If, as is the case in many Roman Catholic churches, there are several readers it is best if all approach together and leave together. In the Roman Catholic Mass the Liturgy of the Word lasts from the end of the opening prayer until the end of the Bidding Prayers. The decision as to when to leave the sanctuary will depend on custom but, if possible, readers and those leading the Prayer of the Faithful should leave together after the prayers.

Getting it together

There is a great advantage in calling together those who are engaged in this important ministry. This can be done either within the parish, as a deanery, or occasionally to have a Diocesan Readers' Day. Such a day should not look only at the practical or technical side of public reading but also at the spiritual aspects of the task of a reader.

In a deanery or a diocese

Occasional Days of Recollection or Days of Quiet can be of enormous benefit. They can help people come to grips with some of the Biblical material itself. If possible these days should therefore contain the three main elements of prayer, Bible study and practicalities. It would not need to be held very frequently but often enough to give people a sense of affirmation in their task and help to do it better.

Here is an outline programme for such a Day held on a diocesan basis.

EXAMPLE

PROCLAIMING THE WORD

10.00	Arrival and coffee
10.30	Introductions
10.45	The Task of a Reader — (talk on practicalities)
11.30	Video (this was an amusing 'home-made' video on how *not* to do it!)
12.00	Plenary session (on practicalities — questions and answers)
12.45	Lunch (picnic style)
1.30	Reading the Bible (methods of Bible study explained)
2.00	This Sunday's Readings (work in parish groups on the next Sunday's readings. A suggested method of looking at them was provided)
3.15	Eucharist (at which the Bishop of the Diocese presided)
4.00	Tea and Depart

This Day was the first of its kind to be held in the diocese. It resulted in a number of follow-up meetings in deaneries for readers. In particular these meetings took a closer look at the Biblical text and how to handle it.

In a parish

Meetings of readers can be very valuable. Getting together in the parish has the added advantage of allowing people to practise in the building they use Sunday by Sunday. Similar topics to those for a Deanery Day can be chosen, or the group may wish to concentrate more on the text of each Sunday's readings.

■ THE PLACE OF THE SERMON

The Second Vatican Council re-affirmed the traditional view of the homily being an integral part of the Liturgy of the Word.

'Readings from Scripture and the chants between the readings form the main part of the liturgy of the word. The homily, profession of faith, and general intercessions or prayer of the faithful expand and complete this part of the Mass.' (General Instruction of the Roman Missal, 33; General Introduction to the Lectionary,11.)

'Through the course of the liturgical year the homily sets forth the mysteries of faith and the standards of the Christian life on the basis of the sacred text. Beginning with the Constitution on the Liturgy, the homily as part of the liturgy of the word has been repeatedly and strongly recommended and in some cases it is obligatory . . . The purpose of the homily is that the spoken Word of God may become a proclamation of God's wonderful works in the history of salvation . . . In explaining the biblical word of God proclaimed in the readings it must always lead the community of faithful so that they may hold fast in their lives to what they have grasped by their faith.' (General Introduction to the Lectionary, 24; this quotes the Constitution on the Liturgy, 52 & 10.)

Most would agree that the sermon or homily should be intimately connected with the readings. However, the reality is often very different from the ideal. For a great many people the homily is a big switch-off. It does not explain the readings or make them relevant. Sometimes there is little connection at all and at others there is a very big gap between the subject of the homily and the real life of the congregation. There appear to be four main problems that must be overcome in order for the Word really to speak to people.

The first problem to be overcome is a mental one. A large number of people do not expect the homily to be relevant. Nor do they expect an exposition of the readings to be very enlightening. There is a mental block which has to be overcome. Secondly, people often feel that any exposition of the Word will be 'over their heads' or too academic. Rather than hearing an exposition of the Word which enlightens and clarifies, they have experienced, all too often, an exposition which confuses. They may well have been put off Scripture already and are confirmed in their thinking Sunday by Sunday. Thirdly, the opposite to this over-academic approach can be true. Some homilies are so vague that they say little at all! It becomes an anecdotal slot in which the preacher, in his or her concern to be relevant, seldom gives people the sustenance they are longing for. Finally, sometimes Scripture is abused during the homily. It is used either as a peg to hang a particular theory on or it is used simply as a proof text to back up what the preacher wants to say. This abuse of Scripture only serves to put people off it altogether and to see it as nothing more than a means of proving a particular point of view.

How, then, can Scripture be expounded well during the homily? This is not a book on the art of preaching, but perhaps it may help simply to give one or two pointers:

1 The preacher must know, pray and live the text before expounding it. That means it is no good looking at the readings late on Saturday night! If the texts are read early in the week they can 'simmer away' for a few days before any written preparation is begun.

2 The preacher must always be aware of the danger of reading into the text a theory which is not there and then twisting the text to fit it.

3 The homily needs to be well-structured, not a rambling of disjointed points. It has been said that a good sermon is like a train. It should have a good engine (to get it going), three main carriages (the main points) and a guard's van (to finish it off well)!

4 The homily is better too short than too long.

5 There must be a good balance between exposition of the Word and present-day

illustrations. Too much of either will make the sermon either too academic or too vague.

6 Any stories or anecdotes must truly fit into the sermon and not be strained.

7 The preacher must be careful about language. So many sermons are full of clichés or specialist theological words that they say little to the listeners.

8 The preacher needs to be careful not to have 'hobby-horses', however worthy, which he or she is always talking about!

The sermon is a marvellous opportunity to explain the readings, but it must be handled well and sensitively if that opportunity is not to be missed. It is a sobering thought that prolonged exposure to bad exposition can prevent people from ever discovering the riches of the Word of God.

■ THE PLACE OF MUSIC

Music is an extremely important part of the liturgy in most local churches. Sometimes it can be the beauty of a cathedral choir which lifts our hearts and minds to God. Sometimes it is the foot-tapping rhythm of modern hymns sung with gusto in a parish church. Sometimes it is a few people struggling away with a psalm during Evensong on a dark winter's evening. Music is an important part of the lives of most people; it has the haunting ability to reach those parts of us which cannot be reached by words or intellectual thought. I have sat in concert halls and watched not the orchestra but the audience. The vast majority were almost certainly not churchgoers, and yet it was clear from their faces that they were experiencing something profoundly spiritual. We use music to express our joys and our sorrows, at times of happiness and at times of grief. In addition music is a communal experience. We make it together and often listen to it together. So, where in all this richness does Scripture fit in?

As in all work with the Bible, creativity is needed here. A great deal can be done with surprisingly few resources. A lot of our music already has a Biblical base. We sing the psalms and many of our hymns have Biblical origins. Unfortunately not all churches have the people around to produce musical excellence, but that should not prevent us from enjoying the music we can manage and discovering the Word of God through it.

Here are some pointers which can help:

1 Look out for specifically Biblical songs or hymns. A good many old favourites and new songs are based on Scripture. Often the implications of this are overlooked. It is possible to help people see that the readings they hear and the hymns they sing are linked, and to discover the Word of God through opening their mouths as well as their ears. In this regard it is important to choose the hymns with the greatest of care. Look carefully at the Sunday readings and try to find music which takes up the same theme.

2 Find out what people like. There needs to be a balance between *only* having old favourites and *only* having new songs. Aim for a good bit of both.

3 When teaching new Scriptural hymns or songs explain the context. This can apply to choirs as well as to the congregation. A couple of sentences about how the hymn links with the readings or the context can do wonders. However, this must be kept short. It is not the time for a sermon!

4 Cassettes of either songs or instrumental music can be of help, especially in parishes with little musical tradition. However, do not over-do cassettes. They are useful occasionally but should be used with care. Sometimes quiet instrumental music as a background to the actual reading can help, but this must be sensitively handled. One of the dangers of using cassette music in church is the tendency to fill up every quiet moment with a tape! On the whole our churches are noisy enough and we should resist the temptation to put on a tape because 'nothing else is happening'. People need silence. Unfortunately, there is almost a fear in some churches of allowing a period of quiet during the service.

5 Use the resources you have. Do not try to do too much or aim too high. Easy-to-sing music done well is much more effective than difficult music sung badly.

■ THE PLACE OF DRAMA

Drama has increasingly been used in many churches as a way of proclaiming the Word during the liturgy. Done well it can have a lasting effect on people and enable them to discover new truths about the Scriptures that they would never have found in any other way. However, if it is used it must be done well. Like music it is better to do a simple drama well rather than try something too complicated. It is possible occasionally to have a group in to do a drama for the parish, but on the whole there is more to be gained by doing it yourself. Good material and scripts are readily available from a number of sources but often parishes prefer to work with the text together and come up with their own work. Again there are some simple guidelines for using drama to proclaim the Scriptures:

1 *Stick to the text*. It is usually best to take a modern translation and use the text as it stands, rather than to alter it. This avoids the danger of putting into the text something that is not there. The presentation may wish to put the text into a modern situation but the words are best left to stand for themselves. If a script is to be used make sure it does not abuse the text.

2 *Be simple*. There is no need for complicated props to do a drama well. Simple props help. Too many cause distraction.

3 *Use movement carefully*. Not too much and not too static. In the same way there should be a good use of colour in the form of clothing and the props used.

4 *Keep the drama short*. Like the homily it is better too short than too long.

5 *Use the whole building.* Use the aisles and have people coming in through the congregation. It helps break down any feeling that this is merely a performance.

6 *Do not over-do the use of drama.* Little and often is the golden rule. Some parishes use drama at specific times, such as on Good Friday or at Christmas, but if it is done each year then it must be different and not become a stale 'tradition'.

7 *Use local talent.* It can be very effective to use people known by the congregation. In all probability there will be hidden talent in the parish!

8 *Remember that the group producing the drama are likely to be the ones who will get the most out of the event.* Thinking through the text and acting it out usually means that people discover it in a new way.

The example given below was used in a local church with few props and no acting experience.

EXAMPLE   THE GOOD SAMARITAN

The group took the parable in Luke 10: 30-37 and used the text exactly as it stood, except for changing the names of the places (Jerusalem and Jericho) and the people. The traveller (an Indian woman) was going from a well-known respectable suburb into the local bus station, notorious for its muggings and vandalism!

The Levite was renamed as a university professor and the Samaritan was a 'punk'.

The text with its changes of names was read by two narrators. The Indian woman entering from the back was 'mugged' silently by a gang of white young men. These appeared from behind pillars etc. and disappeared swiftly. The priest (played by the parish priest) entered from the side and ignored the woman, passing by on his way to say Mass. The university professor, brandishing a large book and wearing an academic gown, swept down the aisle and past the woman without noticing. It was left to the punk rocker to take care of the woman. He picked her up, gave her to a taxi driver and paid the fare. He returned to the centre stage and was joined by the priest and the professor. Which of these three showed mercy? The punk closes the drama with the words, 'Go and do likewise.'

The group chose this familiar story as their first effort and learnt a great deal from the experience. They have since dramatised the Passion Reading on Good Friday and done some drama in the parish outside the setting of the liturgy.

——————————— SECTION 2 ———————————

Adults and Scripture

■ SCRIPTURE AND ADULT FORMATION

This section will look at the role of the Bible in education throughout the parish. We shall look more closely at Scripture and children in the next chapter, so here we shall concentrate mainly on adults. One of the growth areas today in many churches is that of adult education or formation. This, of course, has been part of the life of many traditions for many years. In the past we were often able to assume that those coming into contact with our churches had some awareness of Christianity, however basic. Today that is no longer the case. Many have no background, may know very little and have only the sketchiest (and often misinformed) ideas of what Christianity is all about. Most of these will know little or nothing of the Scriptures except to believe that science has proved it untrue and, consequently, that it is no longer important. The task of forming people in their faith and of helping them to understand what it is all about has, therefore, become more critical. In addition many Christians are unsure of what they think and are feeling somewhat muddled and confused. In the Roman Catholic Church all the changes that have happened since the Second Vatican Council in the 1960s have created a feeling of insecurity for many faithful Catholics. Some have welcomed the changes with open arms and been able to see the value of the more open attitude. Others experience only a feeling of confusion and uncertainty. No longer are they simply being told what to believe and asked to accept it. Now the assumption is that the teaching of the Church should not only be accepted but understood and lived out.

Consequently, there has been a need to give people the opportunity to explore their faith more fully. In addition Roman Catholics have been able to discover the relevance and importance of the Scriptures since the Vatican Council. No longer is the Bible seen as a 'Protestant book' or as a back-up for doctrine. Rather it is increasingly seen as the book all Christians have in common and as a source of nourishment and guidance. However, this opening up of the Scriptures also created the need to have them expounded and explained. People need to know how to handle the Scriptures and use them.

All these changes and new openings have meant that some form of adult education became a necessity rather than just a luxury. The changes also meant that this education must be more than just an acquisition of academic knowledge. It also includes an enrichment of faith and an awareness of how it relates to all areas of our lives. In other words, our work with adults in the parish is about growth in all aspects of their lives.

The awareness that people learn best in smaller groups, and learn from each other, has had its impact on the study of Scripture. The best way of helping people grow in their appreciation of the Scriptures and their understanding of its relevance is not to talk *at* them (however good the talk); it is to allow them to take part in the process of discovery. It is therefore no longer a case of providing the input and pouring it in, like water into an empty bottle. That sort of approach can sometimes lead to the situation in which the notes of the expert pass to the notebooks of the listeners without passing through the minds of either! True Christian learning in all areas, including Scripture, requires a process of 'making it my own'. It involves self-discovery. Naturally this form of helping adults grow in faith is far less tidy and neat than the old method. However, its results are immensely rewarding for everyone. The greatest compliment that can be paid to any teacher is when people say not, 'They taught me this,' but 'We have discovered this for ourselves.' This self-discovery approach applies as much to working with the Bible as with anything else. It always gives me great joy when people come back to me to tell me their stories as to what they have found out *for themselves* about the riches of Scripture.

All this is important because, if we are to interest people in the Bible and help them to explore it, we have to take into account just how people learn. Most adults are quite capable of taking part in serious study or sharing. However, the 'educator' must bear in mind what elements are necessary in adult education. We aim to share with people a living knowledge and love of the Scriptures, so we need to ask, 'What are these people interested in? What do they like to do? What are their interests?' These questions are vital because most adults learn when they have an interest in the subject. They enjoy discovering new truths when these are seen to be interesting and relevant. This applies to most areas of learning, whether it is about the Bible or about cooking or about car mechanics. In practice this means that there is absolutely no point in 'putting on' something if it is not relevant. People will relate to the Bible when they discover how it affects their own lives and that learning about it has a purpose.

There are a number of activities for adults in our parishes in which some form of education takes place. Usually the most helpful learning takes place when people are well motivated. They have discovered a need to know or find out more. Sometimes it is because their children have started to ask questions, or because a new baby has arrived on the scene, and they have appeared at church asking for baptism. Sometimes it is because they have questions of their own for which they want answers. Sometimes they have come up against situations which they find hard to cope with, and they need to sort out their thoughts and feelings in the company of others.

So, all sorts of faith teaching and faith sharing go on in our parishes, some better than others. Here are two situations which involve work with adults and in which Scripture is part of that process. The first example concerns using Scripture in the process of Christian Initiation with adults (pp. 66–69); the second example looks at Scripture in parish organisations (pp. 69–70). Both stress, firstly, the need for people to share together, and secondly, the principle that people learn as much from one another as from the 'leader'. They both show the potential for using Scripture sensibly in our work with adults who are involved in some sort of parish activity.

■ SCRIPTURE IN CHRISTIAN INITIATION

In the Roman Catholic tradition the Rite of Christian Initiation of Adults (RCIA) has given many parishes the opportunity not only to engage as a community in preparing adults to become full members of the Church, but also to revitalise their own faith. A few words of explanation about the RCIA may be helpful here because it has had a profound effect on many local churches. This must of necessity be brief and a fuller treatment can be found in some of the resources recommended at the end of this book. It would perhaps be easiest to describe it as it might operate in a parish, albeit a fictitious one.

The parish of St Cuthbert's used to baptise or receive any new members after a period of instruction by the priest. This usually lasted for about six months and rarely, if ever, involved anyone else. Few knew what was going on or who was present. When the parish took on board the RCIA process it was aware that this was not just a programme but a whole new way of community development. After a good period of preparation by the team (three lay people and the priest) the parish was made fully aware of what it was all about and all were invited to be involved. Everyone had the opportunity to follow the same journey as the candidates. The congregation were directly involved as they welcomed, prayed and shared together their faith story. In this way the RCIA process called forth the whole parish.

In September the first stage of the process began. Meetings were weekly except for holidays. This was the enquiry stage. It was the time for evangelisation and the proclamation of the Gospel. Put simply, this enquiry stage is a time when anyone interested comes along to a parish, is warmly welcomed, and hears the Gospel. In the ancient language of the Church this is the pre-catechumenate stage. The people have the Gospel proclaimed to them, not by being 'preached at', but by sharing stories and by experiencing the Christian community. Ideally, these sessions should contain three main elements:

1 *Sharing experiences* – this is a time for everyone to share their own story or experience related to the subject of the evening;

2 *Input* – a short and precise explanation of the theme;

3 *Liturgy* – this should be short, relevant and non-threatening. It should not be a Eucharist. It can take place at either the beginning or the end of the session.

At St Cuthbert's, those who wished to explore further after this period entered the second phase, the time for deepening faith and for initiation into the ways of prayer and service. They became catechumens. Together with the community they looked at the Scriptures, the Church's stories and the Church today.

At the beginning of Lent the catechumens and the community entered the third stage. The candidates became the Elect and journeyed through a period of prayer and spiritual formation. It was a time of intense preparation and renewal, not just for the candidates, but for the whole parish who had journeyed along with them.

So it was at Easter that the candidates were baptised (if they had not been so before), confirmed and took part for the first time as full members of the Church in the Eucharistic celebration. However, all was not over, for between Easter and Pentecost the community continued to support its new members, who carried on meeting to consider their own ministry and gifts in the Church of Christ.

The Rite of Becoming a Catechumen and the Rite of Election were both celebrated at the main Sunday Mass, and so the whole community entered each stage of the journey with the candidates. This RCIA process is by no means the answer to every prayer as far as adult education is concerned, but it has five major advantages:

- Receiving new members is seen to be the activity of the whole community and it builds up the community.
- Initiation is presented as a journey on which all travel together. It is not a case of the congregation giving and the candidates receiving, but a mutual exploration of our faith. Furthermore, it is not just 'head knowledge' which is involved in this exploration.
- It enables *all* to continue to grow in their faith.
- It is linked strongly with the practice of the ancient Church and, done well, emphasises the place of Scripture.
- It is flexible, and the rule for any parish using RCIA is to adapt it and to go on adapting.

I have outlined the RCIA process because it has a number of things to teach us about using Scripture with adults. Firstly, in the initiation process Scripture can be used in a variety of ways and we have already stressed the importance of variety. It is often used:

- in liturgies which are non-Eucharistic, which meet the needs of the group and can be tailored to the theme;
- in the small-group work in which people are sharing together;
- in the form of drama or role play.

Secondly, RCIA is not a heavy-handed introduction to Scripture. The emphasis is very much on our stories and The Story, an important consideration when working with those unfamiliar with Scripture.

Thirdly, it is (or should be) an integrated and holistic approach whereby Scripture is part and parcel of what is happening. It is not something slotted in at the beginning or tagged on at the end because we feel we ought to have a bit of Scripture in our session somewhere. This has the added 'knock-on' effect of initiating people into an awareness that the Bible should be central and not an optional extra.

Fourthly, parishes are free to develop their own plan of campaign. They can use Scripture in a flexible way and work out a process to meet their own needs. This is a cardinal principle, not just for using the Bible in RCIA but in all situations.

As a practical illustration of how Scripture can be used within the initiation process, here is a session developed by a parish for the first (enquiry) stage. This is their fifth meeting.

ON THE JOURNEY

Think of your life as a road.
On the 'milestones' write down the major events
in your journey through life.
Beside each one, write or draw how
God journeyed with you.

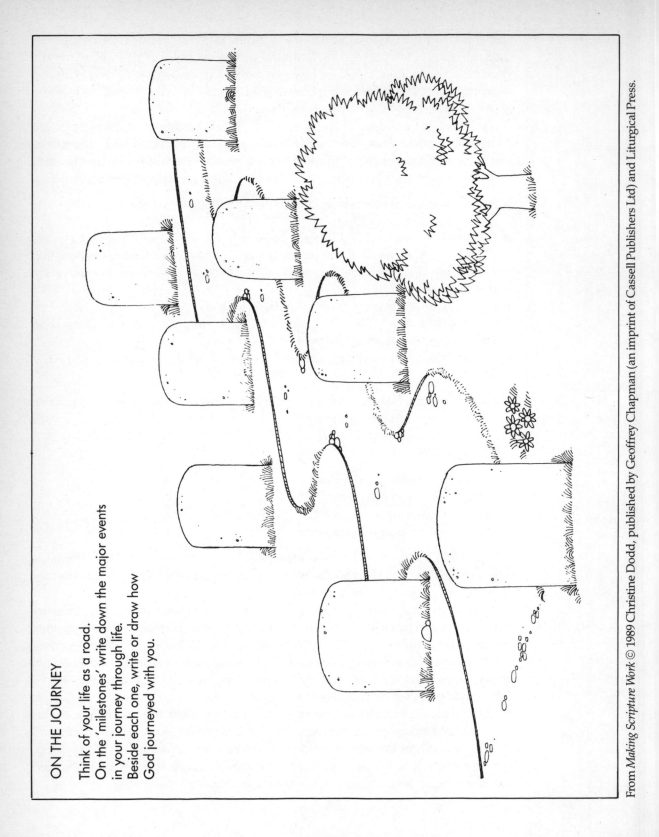

From *Making Scripture Work* © 1989 Christine Dodd, published by Geoffrey Chapman (an imprint of Cassell Publishers Ltd) and Liturgical Press.

EXAMPLE   ON THE JOURNEY

Step 1   Coffee or tea is served as people arrive, allowing time for a general chat.

Step 2   Welcome and opening prayer.

Step 3   Introduction of the theme (by a team member) – Journeying with God.

Step 4   Each person is given the exercise (see page 68) and is asked to fill it in. Allow about ten minutes for people to do this on their own.

Step 5   In small groups participants share what they have done (for this exercise the maximum number in a group should be four).

Step 6   Input (by a team member) on the story of the Exodus.
This should include the following points:
- God is with his people in their hardships.
- God is with them when they wander.
- God is with them in their Joy.
- God is with them always.

Step 7   In small groups participants discuss how God is with them in each of the areas outlined above.

Step 8   Closing liturgy.
- hymn (any hymn with a journey theme, 'Guide me, O thou great Redeemer');
- reading (Exodus 12:31-34, 37-39);
- short silence and closing prayer.

■ SCRIPTURE IN PARISH ORGANISATIONS

There are too many parish organisations and they are too varied to offer something specific for each one. However, by way of example, here is a method used by a well-established part of the parish community – namely the Young Wives' group. In this case the ladies were involved in a good number of parish events. The parish recognised that they were not simply the tea makers or flower arrangers but one of the mainstays of parish life.

They were also concerned to learn more about their faith and about how it related to their task of bringing up families. They met monthly, sometimes for social events, sometimes to hear a speaker, sometimes to discuss among themselves various aspects of their lives. In this case they were considering the question, 'How do we pray at home with the children?'. A speaker was invited to share ideas.

EXAMPLE PRAYER TIME

Step 1   Introductions.

Step 2   What are the difficulties?
What do you do now?
These questions were discussed in a general fashion.

Step 3   The speaker gave a short introduction and example from her own experience.

Step 4   Experiencing a method – (designed for younger children).
(a) Choose a 'Scripture picture' – one for each week.
This is put in the child's bedroom.
Talk about it with the child.
Who are the people and what are they doing?
Perhaps it is possible to light a candle next to the picture.
(b) Use the Bible – ideally this should be kept somewhere special in the child's room (by that we do not mean hidden away!).
A story related to the picture or to the child's day may be read or told.
(c) Pray about the story or passage *as it relates* to the child's experience of the day. Let the child do the praying as well as you.
The candle is blown out.
(Do not overdo this method – perhaps once a week is sufficient.)

Step 5   A discussion of the method, its strengths and weaknesses, was then held.

Step 6   The session ended with a prayer for our families and a cup of tea or coffee.

SECTION 3

Scripture and the Sacraments

We saw earlier how Scripture can be used in the RCIA process. We shall now consider how it can be effective in other forms of preparation for the Sacraments. In particular this section will give examples of using the Bible in preparation for the Baptism of Infants, the Eucharist, Reconciliation and Confirmation. It could also be used for Marriage preparation courses and the Anointing of the Sick. Even if these examples do not directly apply to your tradition the principles they illustrate are necessary in any form of Bible work.

■ SCRIPTURE IN PREPARATION FOR THE BAPTISM OF INFANTS

A good many parishes are now stating that parents and godparents require some form of preparation before the baptism of children. Just how this happens varies tremendously from church to church and tradition to tradition. In some parishes this may be a fairly lengthy process, in others very little is required. Increasingly, this preparation is being done by a team of people rather than the priest or minister alone. There is also a growing awareness that it is best if this happens in a group within the parish rather than just on a one-to-one basis.

Many readers will know that informed preparation of parents was not a common practice within the Roman Catholic Church. There is a saying that we tell against ourselves: 'If it moves, baptise it; if it doesn't bury it!'. Today, however, the scene has shifted considerably and, as more and more parishes see the need for good preparation, so the need for good material becomes apparent. In reality the question has now moved from the theological 'Why should we prepare people?' to the practical 'How shall we do it?'. In response to this need a good many schemes appeared, many parishes developing their own. Yet very few of these had much of a Scriptural element to them, much less gave people an experience of discovering the glories which lie betwen the covers of the Bibles many of them give to their children as a Baptism present.

Mickey and Terri Quinn of Veritas Family Resources pioneered a Baptism preparation programme entitled *Handing on the Faith in the Home*, which has Scripture embodied within it, but in such a way that the elements of Scripture, community and worship all dovetail into one another. As an example of this integrated approach to using Scripture within such a programme, here are elements from the second session of the four-session 'course'. The full material can be found in *Handing on the Faith in the Home* (Veritas Publications, Dublin, 1980).

EXAMPLE

SHARING THE LIGHT

Setting the atmosphere
Place a copy of the Bible (opened at Mark 4:21-23) on a little table in the room in which the meeting is to be held, and have a light lit in front of the open book. This can be done for the third and fourth evenings also, and can help to highlight the importance of the Bible in faith development and the presence of Jesus in the Scriptures.

Step 1a: Welcome and prayer
A word of welcome is usually spoken, followed by a short prayer — perhaps that the parents doing the programme will come to understand better the meaning of their own Baptism and what it involves.

Step 1b: Recap

A second member of the team can do a short recap on the previous evening. Something like:

❙❙Last week we looked at the first stage of the celebration of Baptism – at the door – where the parents and godparents are greeted by the priest and accept the responsibility for handing on their faith to their child. We looked at what handing on faith means and we saw that what God most wants us to do is to love one another. Tonight we are looking at the second big way in which faith is handed on – which is the *example* we give in the home. So tonight we move to the second stage of the celebration of Baptism, to the Book of Scriptures, and you see we have a lit candle before the open Bible on the table. In a very real sense, the Word of God is spoken to children through the example of their parents' lives.❙❙

Step 1c: Involving exercise

It is important, within the first ten minutes of any adult education session, to involve the participants somehow in the process, and this short exercise is not threatening to people who are nervous of having to form a full sentence in a larger group. Have a blank chart on the wall and a felt-tip pen. One member of the team takes responsibility for the exercise. Put down one or two words that you connect with Baptism and ask the parents to add to that. Write them down as they are spoken: baby, priest, white robe, church, family, water, candle, crying, party, photographs, godparents, etc. Then ask if anyone can say which of these words seems most important to them. Put a ring around the words chosen. This puts the parents in contact with some of their notions and feelings about Baptism. Remember this is only a *brief* exercise and should not be used as an opportunity for clarifying or making comments; that can come later.

Step 1d: Outdated notion of Baptism

This brief talk (maximum two minutes) is given by one member of the team. It is quite significant, because it begins to undermine some of the outdated notions which some parents may have. In a few brief words about your new understanding of Baptism, emphasise the role of parents as opposed to a magic ceremony between the baby and God. This little talk should be given by one of the presenting parents and might go something like this:

❙❙The kind of notion of Baptism I grew up with is that Baptism was a private ceremony, between God and the baby, and I didn't think parents or others, apart from the priest, played any real part in it. It was almost something magic – you used water and the correct words and the soul was suddenly whitened and original sin wiped away. The emphasis, in fact, was on 'rules', on doing the right things. Now, I would tend to see Baptism less as a magic change and more as a beginning, like a little seed of faith being planted in the child that depends for its growth on how the parents themselves live. In other words, as I see it now, God works through us parents in strengthening a child's faith.❙❙

Step 2: Focus

The priest or team leader highlights the significance of the second stage of the ceremony of Baptism – at the book of Scriptures. Little need be said at this stage about the Scriptures; this is not a course on Bible study and the main emphasis of the evening is on some updating on Baptism, stressing the parents' role and the importance of their example in the home. The entire talk should not exceed five minutes and might go something like this:

❛❛Last week we heard about the catechumens – the adults in the early Church who wanted to be baptised. They were anointed with oil and began a long period of instruction and formation. That instruction taught them, above all, to appreciate the Bible and to see its importance in their own lives. So it is only right that, for the second stage of the celebration of Baptism, the family moves up from the door, where last week we saw them welcomed, and gathers around the Book of the Scriptures. There they listen to a few passages and a short talk.

I would like to think that the Bible, and especially the Gospels would become more important in your lives too. Quite a few families now read the Sunday Gospel on Saturday evening and ask themselves questions like, 'When did I experience something like that?', 'Who do I like/dislike in that story?', 'How could I be more like Jesus was in that incident?'

So we are going to listen to a very short passage from Scripture now . . . ' (*name*) will you read these few lines please?' Mark 4:21-23 is read. Well, that's a very short passage – about the importance of letting your light shine, so let's just look for a moment at the idea of *light*. Jesus, as you know, described himself as the light of the world and this big Paschal candle with its five wounds stands for Jesus. You will see it lit during your child's Baptism and at one very meaningful moment you will take your child's baptismal candle up to the Paschal candle and light it as the priest prays that you will keep the flame of faith alive in your child's heart.

So we are being asked as parents to let your light shine, to let your children see the example of your own lives. And that's what we want to zone in on tonight – the example you give in your home by the way you live. For it's not much use saying, 'Don't interrupt' if *you* interrupt, or 'Don't criticise' if *you* criticise. Your child will learn the *real* lesson from what you *do* rather than from what you say.❜❜

Step 3: Talk by parents

The purpose of this talk is to highlight the power of the parents' example, both good and bad, on their children. Instances of bad example could include: nagging, criticising, huffing, impatience, complaining, being lazy, thoughtless, greedy, etc. Instances of good example could include: being appreciative, thoughtful, patient, cheerful, other-centred, asking forgiveness, etc. But be *specific*; talk about the hours spent in front of the television set rather than say, 'I'm often lazy'. And show the *effect* of your example on the children.

Point out the *effect* of this example – how the children actually imitate your nagging, your impatience, your interrupting, etc. Also show the effect of this behaviour on the atmosphere in the home, which is so important to a young baby; you could point out how your toddler senses when something is wrong, comes over and hugs your leg, wants to be lifted up, or whatever. End on a positive note, giving some examples of how good example has affected your children (and maybe how *their* example has helped *you*). You could mention how they noticed or imitated your thoughtfulness, truthfulness, honesty, gentleness. Give specific examples. This talk should not go over eight minutes, probably with each parent just speaking once.

It is important always to round off a talk, tying it together and linking it in with the topic of the evening.

Step 4: Handout

A handout is given out with pens, read aloud as the parents mark it off, discussed in pairs and then in small groups, as on the previous night. If the team gave the feedback from each group on the first evening try to ensure that one of the participants gives the feedback this evening.

Ask for the feedback to be as snappy as possible, mentioning that there is no need to repeat what has been said by another group spokesperson. When summing up, clarify just one or maybe two points, but be sensitive — do not contradict what has been said.

Step 5: Prayer Service

The leader now performs the prayer service. A candle is distributed to each couple as a gift from the parish and the lights are put out, leaving only the Paschal candle lit (or another suitable large candle). The leader now lights the small candle for each of the couples in turn, saying each time:

'Receive the light of Christ, (*name*); this light is entrusted to you to be kept burning brightly. Your child will be enlightened by Christ.'

When the last candle has been distributed, the priest finishes the prayer:
'May your children walk as children of light. May the flame of faith be alive in their hearts. When the Lord comes, may they meet him with all the saints in heaven.'
Finally music is played softly in the background (the lights are still out).

■ SCRIPTURE AND RECONCILIATION

With a small group

The setting

This method was used as part of a four-session programme looking at the Sacrament of Reconciliation. It took place during Lent and was used with mature adults but could also be adapted for use by youth groups. The same format was used each time in small groups. In this case the group met in the home of one of the members but there is no reason why it should not be a parish activity meeting in church premises with a larger group splitting into smaller units. This is Session Three, the group having already looked at 'What is the problem' and 'Coming home with others'. This session is entitled 'Coming home to God'.

You will need:
- a copy of the material given here
- pen or pencil for everyone
- Bibles.

Aim
The aim of this session is to help us see what 'falling out' with God means.

EXAMPLE

COMING HOME

Coming together
Individually, look back over the past week and then complete the following:

'I felt joyful this week when...'

'I felt I had failed this week when ....'

Now take your answers and share with one other person.

Prayer
A member of the group leads the opening prayer.

Read
Another person reads Luke 18:9-14 slowly.

Exploring the Jesus story
Discuss together:

- The Pharisee led a good, moral, upright life. What was his main problem?
- The Publican was not considered an upright citizen in society, yet he was commended. Why do you think this was?
- What does the story say about the word 'sin'?

How would you, as a group, define sin? Try to write your definition here in not more than one short sentence.

....

....

Now for ourselves
Jot down here:

Who am I most like in the story? ....

When?...

How do I personally often 'fall out' with God?...

Discuss what you have written with one or two other people.
Now come back together and talk for a few moments about how you think we can be reconciled to God.

Conclusions
Have we any conclusions (one member jots them down):

- about how we could help one another?
- about our attitude when we 'fall out' with God?
- about our attitude when we want to 'come home'?

Reflection
In a few moments of silence ask yourself, 'What does God see as the most damaging attitude in my life?'

Closing Prayer
One person reads Psalm 51:1-13
All: Our Father . . .

Notes
1. Advantages of the method:
   (a) There is plenty of variety in the method (working alone, in pairs, together). This helps everyone to be involved.
   (b) The leader is seen very much as a facilitator rather than an 'expert'. There is no need for a specialist to be present.
2. Points of importance:
   (a) Make sure everyone in the group is happy to do writing and comfortable with it.
   (b) Notice the way the method moves:
       our life → Scripture → reflection on our lives.
   (c) The time of reflection at the end helps people assimilate what they have learnt and relate it to their daily life.

Community celebration

In addition to the work in small groups on the theme of reconciliation, Scripture can be used as the basis for reconciliation services for the whole Christian community. The example given here was used in Passiontide as a penitential service in a Roman Catholic parish. It therefore includes a time for individual confession. Those in other denominations where this is not part of their tradition could still use the basis of this service, allowing simply a time of meditation instead of sacramental reconciliation.

The Service is based on the story of Jesus in Gethsemane and this is used as a focus for the meditation.

EXAMPLE

HIS SORROW – OUR JOY
(A Lenten Service of Reconciliation)

This evening we shall look at the Passion of Christ and, in particular at His agony in the Garden of Gethsemane. This will form the focus for our thoughts and prayers which will be of a reflective nature.

There will be several periods of silence during the Service so please either sit or kneel – whichever is the most comfortable for you.

Processional hymn

Introduction and Opening Prayer

Leader Father, our source of life
You know our weakness.
May we reach out with joy to grasp your hand
And come with trust to receive your forgiveness.
We ask this through Jesus Christ our Lord
Who died that we might live

All Amen.

Reading Matthew 26:36-46

(A period of silence will now be kept in which we can place ourselves in the presence of Jesus in Gethsemane. Some music will follow.)

Hymn *(Please remain seated)*

All 1. Were you there when they crucified my Lord?
Were you there when they crucified my Lord?
Sometimes it causes me to tremble, tremble, tremble.
Were you there when they crucified my Lord?

2. Were you there in the garden when he prayed?

3. Were you there, did you see his agony?

4. Were you there when he found his friends asleep?

Examination of Conscience

Reader 1 Stay here and keep watch with me.
Reader 2 When have we failed to stay awake with Christ?
Reader 1 Stay here and keep watch with me.
Reader 2 When have we slept and failed to listen to God?
Reader 1 Stay here and keep watch with me.
Reader 2 When have we slept and failed to let ourselves be prompted by the Holy Spirit?

Reader 1 Stay here and keep watch with me

Reader 2 When have we slept and failed to hear the voice of our own conscience.

Reader 1 Stay here and keep watch with me.

Reader 2 When have we failed to truly trust in God?

Reader 1 Stay here and keep watch with me.

Reader 2 When have we failed to be humble?

Reader 1 Stay here and keep watch with me.

Reader 2 When have we failed to let God into our lives?

Reader 1 Stay here and keep watch with me.

Reader 2 When have we failed to change our behaviour?

Reader 1 Stay here and keep watch with me.

Reader 2 When have we failed to see God in others?

Reader 1 Stay here and keep watch with me.

Reader 2 When have we failed to give generously to the others?

Reader 1 Stay here and keep watch with me.

Reader 2 When have we slept and failed to help those who needed our care?

Following this examination of conscience we shall spend a short time reflecting on our own lives.

The Presentation of the Cross

Jesus journeyed from Gethsemane to Calvary. A cross is now presented as an aid to our meditation. It reminds us of the length to which the love of God for us will go.

(Either: a period is now allowed for individual confession – during this time a selection of readings and songs should be offered. Or: time is allowed for personal reflection and meditation)

Closing Prayer

Leader Father of all light

Father of all mercy

Father of all forgiveness

For your compassion we thank you

For your love we thank you

For your light we thank you.

Send us out in your world so that when others are in Gethsemane we may be a light in their darkness.

We ask this through Jesus Christ our Lord.

Amen.

All **Hymn**

With children preparing for First Communion

The Setting

This example comes from a parish introducing children to reconciliation as part of preparation for their first Holy Communion. The children were aged seven to eight. They came weekly and parents came with them once a month. Usually this was a Sunday afternoon (fairly late to allow the Sunday lunch to go down!). During this time the parents, and sometimes a grandparent or sponsor if the home situation required it, were able to see what the children were doing. They worked through the same theme as the children so that they could answer any questions at home. They were given ideas and material for use during the month and were informed of exactly what the children would be doing in the next three weeks. Many parishes found that parents learn more about their own faith doing this than they have done for years. In the following example the parents and children are together looking at the theme of 'saying sorry'. They sit in family groups. They have been asked to bring with them a picture of their home.

You will need
- Copies of the illustrations on page 81 are needed, one for each family
- pens or pencils
- outline of the wall and the 'bricks' to stick on. (This can be done with sticky tape)
- large felt pen
- the sheet of the outline house, one for each family
- drawing of the red and blue saucepan (or copy of page 80) for the story
- a picture of your own house
- large sheets of paper and felt pens for mounting pictures of children's houses.

EXAMPLE   THE WALL

Coming together
As families arrive the pictures they have brought are mounted and each family writes underneath, ' . . . (child's name) house'. These are put up around the walls of the room for all to see.

The story
Short input by a member of the team.

Discuss the children's photos. What do you like about your house? What don't you like?

❛❛Here is my house. I live in it along with . . . Lots of things live in it as well. In my cupboard live two saucepans, a red one and a blue one. (Show picture of red saucepan as shown.)

The red saucepan always frowns because it hates being used. He says, 'They scrub me, put hot things in me, sit me on a hot flame.' He is grumpy.

(Show picture of blue saucepan, as shown.) The blue saucepan says, 'They fill me with lovely things to eat. I feel useful. They wash me lovely and clean afterwards.' She is happy.

We are often like the saucepans, sometimes grumpy, sometimes happy.❜❜

Family activity
Here are some frowning faces. Why do you think they are frowning?

Each family is given a sheet of 'frowning faces' and has to write down a time someone in the family has done or said these things. (Allow about ten minutes.)

From *Making Scripture Work* © 1989 Christine Dodd, published by
Geoffrey Chapman (an imprint of Cassell Publishers Ltd) and Liturgical Press.

FROWNING FACES

From *Making Scripture Work* © 1989 Christine Dodd, published by
Geoffrey Chapman (an imprint of Cassell Publishers Ltd) and Liturgical Press.

Input

The leader now talks about the times we are grumpy or unkind. He or she asks the children, or the adults, to call out the worst of attitude we have when we say, 'It's mine,' or 'Why should I?' or 'I hate you.' As the answers are called out the leader or a team member writes them down on one of the 'bricks' and sticks them onto the wall. The leader stresses that these attitudes separate us from each other and from God. Like a wall they prevent us from getting close to one another and to God. They cut us off. We have to knock down the wall, or rather we have to allow someone to knock it down for us. The wall is knocked down when we say 'sorry' (go through saying 'sorry' for each of the bricks on the wall, taking them down as you go).

Now we need to build a new house. It needs to be strong and secure. It will need good foundations. Ask the children what sort of things make a good foundation for a house. Ask the adults what sort of attitudes make a good foundation for life.

Reading

Matthew 7:24-27. This should be read from a translation suitable for the age of the children. If time allows it could be dramatised.

Conclusion

Sing *The Wise Man Built His House Upon The Rock.*

■ SCRIPTURE AND PREPARATION FOR CONFIRMATION

The setting

This example, on the theme of living Christ today, was used with a group of Confirmation candidates aged sixteen but it could be adapted for use with a younger group. There were ten youngsters in the group and three adults. The material comes from one of the books in the Teenagers Talking series by Moira Leigh, *Teenagers talking* (The Grail, 1978).

Aim

To show that Christianity is not just a 'religion' but a way of life.

EXAMPLE   LIVING CHRIST TODAY

Notes for leader

Make a collection of pictures which illustrate being 'constructive' and 'destructive', e.g. pictures of buildings, bridges, etc., then of bombed cities, broken china, etc.

Introduce the meeting by explaining these illustrations and then asking the group the question: Which is the easiest to do, to build or destroy?

Then go on to say that similarly in our conversation and our attitudes towards people, it is much easier to break down and destroy others by ignoring them, mocking them, saying unkind things about them, than it is to 'build up' another person.

Christ told his apostles, 'The mark by which all men will know you for my disciples will be the love you bear one another.' The characteristic of the Christian must be his ability to love and 'build up' other people.

Practical activities

Ask the group to think about the things that destroy human relations:

1 Write down the type of conversation at school and at home which destroys.

2 Pick out items in the newspaper which indicate the destruction of human relationships.

3 Discuss the type of entertainment which shows the breakdown of family life.

Three situations

In order to concentrate more on the 'building up' of human relations in everyday life, it is suggested that the group is divided into three, and each small group given one of the following to work on:

1. Turn the conversation

So much of the conversation one hears is destructive rather than constructive. Write down the sort of remarks which help to 'build up' people.

Act some scenes demonstrating how you turn a conversation or change an attitude towards someone. (Give the group some lead-in with something like the following: 'Here comes John with Sarah. I can't imagine what he sees in her at all . . .' or, 'I have never met her, but someone told me in confidence that . . .').

2. The charity of good manners

Are good manners simply an outward display or can they be an expression of love and respect? What qualities are involved in good manners? Draw up a list of what you consider most important in showing good manners at the present time. Illustrate these by acting, drawing or writing a limerick.

3. The acid test

Today everything is put to the test. People don't take your word for it; they want scientific proof.

If the test of a Christian is his attitude toward other people, what would you be looking for? You would expect a Christian to act as Christ acted towards his friends, his enemies, the sick etc.

Take each of the following Scriptural passages and decide what each one is telling us about Christ's attitude towards other people and what this can teach us today in our relations with other people:

Luke 10:25-37 – The Good Samaritan
John 13:4-10 – Jesus washes his apostles' feet
John 8:3-11 – The woman taken in adultery
Matt 18:21-35 – The unforgiving servant.

Decide on one of these examples and 'get it over' to the rest of the group in some way when you come together. This can be done by direct explanation or by a folk song or ballad.

Thought
'Today the Christian man and the Christian woman will be the only Bible that the vast majority of people will ever read.'

Perhaps an example from a contemporary person's life which illustrates the theme of practical Christianity could be given: e.g. Mother Teresa, Group Captain Cheshire.

SECTION 4

Scripture and Pastoral Care

■ PARISH VISITING

In the pastoral care work in our parishes we are often dealing with people who are very vulnerable. The sick, the lonely, the bereaved, the depressed all face problems which can make them feel alienated from the world in which they live. Such people often welcome a visit from the church but the visitors are sometimes at a loss to know what to do or to say. Increasingly, parishes are giving those who undertake pastoral care a little basic help. Often this is no more than they already know. Most of it is common sense but much can be gained from such meetings. It gives people confidence in themselves and their role as well as some guidelines about how to react and handle the situation. Scripture can be used in two ways to help the visitors. Firstly it can help them to explore the basis for the work they undertake. Secondly they can discover how to use Scripture with the people they visit and the importance of using it sensitively and carefully.

There are, of course, many situations in which Scripture could be used, but here are just two. The first was used with a group of people who were in contact with the bereaved, and the second with a group who primarily ministered to the housebound. In both cases the Bible is used in a training session but in the second the emphasis is on how to use the Scriptures with the people being visited.

Looking at grief

This was the first of six sessions looking at bereavement. It was used with a group of ordinary people from the parish who did general pastoral visiting but who often found themselves with bereaved people. The group consisted of nine adults and met in the house of one of the members. Everyone already knew one another quite well.

EXAMPLE

After a general chat over coffee, and when everyone was relaxed, the meeting began with a short period of silent prayer. Quiet background music was played. One of the group opened with a short prayer.

Step 1 People were asked to call out what they hoped for from the sessions. These were written up (one or two words for each contribution) on a large sheet of paper. No discussion was allowed at this point.

Step 2 When everyone who wished had contributed there was a general discussion about what had emerged.

Step 3 The leader suggested that the group look at grief situations.

What are these? Again people were asked to contribute and a list was made. The aim was to draw out from people that death is not the only reason for a sense of bereavement.

The list included examples such as loss of a job, separation from a family, loss of a limb, divorce, loss of health.

Step 4 In pairs the participants were asked to share their own experience of bereavement. People were encouraged to tell the story and to say how it *felt* at the time rather than to intellectualise about it.

Step 5 The group as a whole discussed the feelings which had emerged: anger, guilt, despair, how can God let this happen?

Step 6 Psalm 88 was then read slowly and a short silence kept.

Step 7 The group considered the psalm by looking at the feelings of the psalmist.
- What does the psalmist seem to feel?
- What images does the psalmist use to express these feelings?
- What images do people use today: are they the same or different?

Step 8 The psalm was read again. A silence was kept for a while and a final prayer closed the session.

(Group members were encouraged to take the psalm and try to rewrite it using modern-day images which express feelings of grief.)

Note: the close link between Scripture and the subject under discussion. It is not dragged in to make a point but to help people express what they feel.

Looking at prayer

The setting

The group using this example were involved in general parish visiting – often of the housebound. The session looked at the sensitive question of whether or not to pray with people and using the Bible with them. It was the subject at one of the regular meetings held by the group to plan and discuss their activity. The meeting was held in a small church hall and took the form of a role play followed by a discussion and some input.

EXAMPLE   TO PRAY OR NOT TO PRAY

Step 1   After everyone was present and settled the role play was used. It was in two parts. Four characters were required: two visitors and the two people to be visited.

Step 2   Two people volunteered and were given the following information (for their eyes only).

Mr (or Mrs) Phillips

You are an elderly person, mentally active but now physically unable to get about much. You have always been an active church-goer and welcome a visit. You receive Communion at home regularly but you are also pleased when someone calls at other times. You have the parish intercession paper and pray for those mentioned each day.

Mrs (or Mr) Holt (visitor)

You are an experienced visitor and know Mr (or Mrs) Phillips well. You know a chat is always welcome and that he or she is a prayerful person, so a short prayer and reading would be welcomed.

Step 3   Allow the visitor to make the visit for about ten minutes. Once the role play is over remember to 'de-role' the participants.
Draw out from them how they felt:
● How could they have dealt with the situation differently?
● What did they find difficult?

Step 4   Now allow the other two people to role play. Give them the following information (again for their eyes only).

Mrs (or Mr) Allan

You are a middle-aged person, but crippled with arthritis and so unable to get about. You have never had much connection with the church but you always watch *Songs of Praise* on television and say your prayers. You welcome the visitor, though you feel you need to keep stressing why you never went often when you were fit. You also stress that you pray a lot. Deep down you would welcome the visitor to pray with you or read a passage of Scripture. However you are too embarrassed to ask for this directly.

Mr (or Mrs) Harris (visitor)

You have only met Mrs (or Mr) Allan once before. You know he or she has never been a regular church-goer but is very sympathetic. He or she 'says me prayers ev'ry day'.

Step 5   Once again allow about ten minutes and then discuss with the participants how they felt, what they found difficult, and how the situation could have been helped.

Step 6   Now have a general discussion about what happened and about the joys and difficulties of praying with others and using Scripture with them.

Step 7   Input.

Make sure the following points are covered. They will probably have emerged from the group but it is good to reinforce and clarify them.

- Above all, sensitivity to the needs of the person is required.
- The visitor must be able to discern whether or not a prayer or reading would be welcomed.
- *Only* use Scripture if it is clear the person really wants this.
- The visitor will need to have some idea of suitable passages.
- For those who would welcome a reading the visitor will need to discern if people would just like it read, or want to discuss it, or would rather a text was suggested for them to read themselves later.
- Keep it short.
- Do not preach or explain the reading – let it speak for itself.
- The visitor will need to discern on EACH VISIT if the person would like a prayer or reading. Never assume that because you have done it once it will always be welcomed.
- People must be given the opportunity to say no without difficulty.

Step 8   The meeting ended with coffee.

Scripture and Evangelisation

Evangelisation

Evangelisation is a difficult word for many. For some it conjures up pictures of mass rallies, American evangelists or pressure tactics. To others it is solely the concern of those who go overseas or those special people who come to hold a parish mission. To some it means speaking directly and overtly about the Gospel. To others it chiefly means setting a good example. Because there are so many different interpretations of the word it would be good if we could cease to use it altogether for a while and find some other expression, perhaps 'sharing our faith' or 'telling our story'.

Most effective evangelisation happens through our relationships with others. It is what we are, how we act and what we say to the people who know us which is the primary means of sharing our faith. Unfortunately this is not always recognised, and in many local churches people tend to assume that only specialised people can engage in any form of faith sharing. There is, of course, a place for the parish mission or the special event but this is not the bread and butter of faith sharing. Indeed the greatest effect of many parish missions is not the number of new people whom we contact but the encouragement given to many of the regular church-goers to be more effective in their own faith sharing.

If people are to share their faith they need, above all, affirmation: the confidence that they can, and will, be used by God. Most of our churches need both to help people believe that faith sharing is necessary and to give them the confidence to do it. Many of us, therefore, need to look at the whole subject of evangelisation: what it means, why it is important, and where we fit in. We must explore what evangelisation does and does not mean. In this process of equipping people to share faith, gentleness and patience are necessary. Some will take to it like a duck to water; others will find faith sharing far more problematical.

As far as faith sharing in the parish is concerned we must keep four major points in mind:

1. *Evangelisation is not about results.* The task of the Christian community is to proclaim the Gospel faithfully. The results of and response to that proclamation should not be our major concern. What is important is that we listen openly to the Word of God and deliver his message faithfully.

2. *Evangelisation is not about methods.* Techniques, methods and programmes may be a part of the process but faith sharing should be a natural part of our life in Christ and not something special we have to do every so often.

3. *Evangelisation is NEITHER solely about giving a good example NOR solely about speaking of our faith in words.* It is, or should be, a combination of both. Words without example will reach no one, and at times verbal communications or explanations are necessary.

4. *Scripture is important in this process,* provided that it is used sensibly. In the past the Bible has been used in evangelisation in many ways which have not always been to our credit. It has sometimes been used to 'bludgeon' people, or to 'proof text' a particular version of Christianity. To our shame it has sometimes been employed as a means of answering all awkward questions or even to frighten people into rethinking their position. How, then, should Scripture be used?

Generally Scripture is best used as a help and guide to Christians in their faith sharing. It is *our* resource book, not one we should expect others immediately to understand or comprehend. 'Gently does it' is the golden rule for all Biblical work in this area. We are engaged in proclaiming to others what God is like and what he means to us. Ramming Scripture down their throats is not sharing the Good News. First there must be mutual sharing and dialogue for *both* parties.

Here is one example of how to explore what the Good News means both in Scripture and for today. It was used by a group engaged in thinking through their own attitudes and responses to faith sharing.

EXAMPLE　　## OUR GOSPEL

Step 1　The group began with a short prayer.

Step 2　St Paul talks about 'my Gospel' (2 Tim 2:8). Put into your own words, without using any technical jargon, what YOUR Gospel is. What is the Good News for you? Do this individually, writing down just one or two sentences.

Step 3　Pool your responses. What are the main themes you have in common?

Step 4　In the early days of Christianity evil powers were considered very real, and therefore the thrust of the Gospel was concerned with the victory of Christ over them. What is the main problem today, and what is the cutting edge of the Gospel for our age?

Step 5　Read Mark 1:14-39.
- In what ways does Jesus proclaim the Kingdom of God?
- How does he share Good News?
- Why was it effective?
- What have we to learn from the passage?

Step 6　In preparation for next time see if you can find out from friends or acquaintances what they think the Church is for.

Step 7　Closing prayer.

CHILDREN, YOUNG PEOPLE AND SCRIPTURE

IN THIS CHAPTER we shall be looking at the use of Scripture with both children and young adults. It is a sad reflection on our churches and schools that so many people have grown up with such a poor view of what the Bible is about. A good number feel that, as children, they were not introduced to Scripture in a meaningful way. Their experiences were often boring and irrelevant. Consequently they have grown up misunderstanding the role and the richness of the Scriptures. The guidelines and practical examples given in this chapter are intended to enable our children to grow up with a much more positive attitude to the Bible.

SECTION 1

Children and Scripture

Basic principles

It cannot be denied that using Scripture with children is difficult. The Bible is primarily an adult book. That is not to say that it cannot be opened to children or that they should not be encouraged to use it. However, we must realise that a good deal of it will not be relevant to them and, therefore, that we should handle it with care. Using the Bible well with children is vital because so many wrong seeds can be sown in a young life. If the Scriptures are used wrongly or abused, this will have to be unlearnt and rebuilt in the future, while if we encourage the right attitudes at an early age, the Word of God can be a means of growth in faith throughout life. It cannot be stressed strongly enough that opening up the Bible to children is more than just story-telling. We must aim primarily to instill basic attitudes of what Scripture is for, respect and reverence for the Word and a growing awareness that it is relevant to our lives. How, then, can we use the Bible sensibly and sensitively with children? Before looking at some examples a few basic 'dos and don'ts' should be mentioned which must be borne in mind, however we use the Bible with children.

1 *Children need to pick up a reverence for Scripture.* They will often do this by watching adults and noticing the attitude of those around them. The Bible should not be treated as just any old book, nor even as a special book of special stories. It is a living record which still speaks. It contains our rich heritage which stretches back beyond Jesus to our roots in Judaism. Seeing the Bible given a place of honour, reverently handled and used for prayer can have a lasting influence. It can help to have a good illustrated Bible on display, carefully set up, so that the children can see as well as hear its riches.

2 *Relevance of Scripture.* To say that education is more than simply bombarding children with information sounds too obvious to need stating and yet this is often what happens with regard to the Bible. We want them to know what is in it, who

came from, what they did and how they did it. Some factual knowledge is obviously necessary, but this is not ALL there is to it. The aim of using Scripture with children people were and where they came from, what they did and how they did it. Some factual knowledge is obviously necessary, but this is not ALL there is to it. The aim of using Scripture with children is not only to give them Biblical knowledge but also to help them relate the Biblical message to their own lives. For this reason it is necessary to respect the interaction that takes place between the everyday life of the child and the Bible.

3 *We should aim at letting the Bible speak for itself and not always be speaking about the Bible.* Too often the teacher places more emphasis on his or her own interpretation of the Bible's message for the children than on letting the children discover an interpretation for themselves.

4 *We should keep a balance between going overboard with the Bible and not using it at all.* Too much of it will mean that it becomes forced and unnatural. Too little and the message given is that it is not important at all.

5 *We need to be selective in what we use:* to take into account the age range of the children and the stage of development they have reached. Using texts which are unsuitable or too difficult is likely to create problems both for the present and for the future. Parables, for instance, should be very carefully used. They are designed to raise questions in the minds of the listeners. If used wrongly they become little more than an example of good living, open to only one interpretation; and so the children quickly pick up the impression that there is only one purpose to a parable and only one reason for its existence.

6 *Pray with Scripture.* In this way the children see in action that it is a living book and not just a collection of stories from the past. However, praying with the Bible must be carefully done and be natural and not forced.

If those are the 'do's', here are the 'don'ts' for handling the Bible with children.

1 *Don't use the Bible to threaten children.* This is 'the Bible says you mustn't' or 'the Bible says you must' attitude. Using the Bible in this authoritarian way is to misuse it, and it is bound to change what should be an adventure of discovery for the children into a bondage.

2 *Don't take heroes from the Bible and make them out to be supermen!* Remember that the great figures of the Bible are set within communities and cannot be isolated from them.

3 *Don't be too rigid in your use of Scripture.* Include a variety of presentations and methods: action as well as words, drama as well as story, art and dance, poetry and song.

4 *Don't make the Bible too 'spiritual'.* It must relate to the ordinary life of the children.

5 *Don't underestimate the children's ability to take on board what Scripture is saying.* It is important, of course, to answer children's questions and to do so honestly. Somehow it is important to keep the balance so that Scripture is neither too difficult to cope with nor too babyish to be interesting.

The examples which follow look at three areas in which Scripture can be used with children. There are others, of course, but these three should give a good idea of what can be achieved.

■ SCRIPTURE IN THE HOME

It has to be admitted that many parents experience difficulties in knowing how to use the Bible at home with their children. Some of these difficulties are practical ones, such as how to get the whole family together at one time or how to involve everyone of whatever age. Other difficulties are more subtle: what to do when friends come to stay who may not be used to such a practice, or how to keep it natural and yet powerful. We require something which is symbolically powerful, socially unembarrassing, simple and practical. It is not easy to discover what or how. There are, however, times in the year which lend themselves to special Bible work. The major seasons of Advent and Lent can be marvellous opportunities for the family to prepare together for the festivals. We can use these seasons to involve everyone in some sort of family home liturgy in which Scripture plays an important part.

Here is one example, worked out by a group of parents for use in the home during Holy Week. Like all work with the Bible, using Scripture at home requires variety and creativity. Doing the same old thing day in and day out is more likely to put the children off than to give them a love for the Bible. This example helps to bring out the importance of symbol and variety. It is not something that could be done every week. It is powerful because it is special and because it links in with this special week in the Church's year.

I am grateful to the Rev H. Dickinson for his permission to use this material and to the parents in his parish who pioneered it.

EXAMPLE   A HOME LITURGY FOR HOLY WEEK

Introduction
These liturgies took place in the home around the table at a mealtime. Breakfast or the evening meal seemed to work out best for most families but it will depend on personal circumstances.

What you need
- A circular disc with six candle holders around the edge and one in the centre.
- Six white candles and one red candle.
- The various symbols listed below and a Bible.

PALM SUNDAY

Light six candles (the central place is left empty).

A palm cross from church should be on the table.

Sing (if confident): *Sing Hosanna to the King of Kings* or any Palm Sunday hymn.

Reading: Mark 11:1-11.

Question from child: 'Why do we have six candles and this palm cross on the table today?'

Answer: 'Because today Jesus had only six more days to live and all the people welcomed him into Jerusalem waving palm branches.'

MONDAY

Light five candles.

At the centre a prayer book or missal stands open at the Lord's Prayer (or children can copy out the Lord's Prayer in different languages in their best writing).

A knotted cord.

Reading: Mark 11:15-19.

Question from child: 'Why do we have five candles and the Lord's Prayer on our table today?'

Answer: 'Because Jesus has only five more days to live. Today he threw the money changers out of the temple and said it should be a worship place for everyone. Instead he gave us the Our Father as prayer for everybody everywhere.'

TUESDAY

Light four candles.

At the centre a twig of dead wood.

Reading: Mark 11:12-14 and 20-25.

Question from child: 'Why do we have four candles and a dead twig on our table today?'

Answer: 'Because Jesus has only four days to live. Today he showed how people die if they get separated from God.'

(John 15 is obviously appropriate.)

WEDNESDAY

Light three candles.

At the centre, a fine porcelain jar.

Reading: Mark 14:1-9.

Question from child: 'Why do we have three candles and a china jar on our table today?'

Answer: 'Because Jesus has only three days to live. He told us that if we wanted to do something to help him in his Passion we should do it by giving to the poor.'

(Everyone present puts some of their own money into the jar.)

THURSDAY

Light two candles.

There are a number of alternative options here. If a Christian Passover meal is going to be held then a towel and bowl can be the symbols. If not, a glass of wine and a bread roll could be used.

Reading: Mark 14:17-26. Appropriate explanation.

FRIDAY

Light one candle and then blow it out.

Symbols of the Passion – nails, vinegar, a sponge, a hammer, some plaited brambles.

Pin the palm cross to the front door of house.

Reading: Mark 15:21-30. Appropriate explanation.

SATURDAY

The family together make an Easter Garden. No candles are lit.

Reading: Mark 15:42-47.

EASTER DAY

Light the seven candles (one tall red one in the middle) along with one by the empty tomb in the Easter Garden.

One Easter present for each member of the family.

Reading: Mark 16:1-7. Appropriate explanation.

It is important to keep it light and active – not too much heavy explanation. A good deal of adaptation can be made to the basic scheme depending on the age of the children. It is also important to have as much time as possible available so that the process is not rushed.

This example is taken from the Bible Reading Fellowship *Ladder Books* (weekly activities for children in five age groups) and is designed for use by children either on their own or with an adult.

There are three important points to note about this method. Firstly, the Biblical references are short, just one or two verses for this age group (seven to twelves). Secondly, there is interaction between the Scriptures and the child's real life. Thirdly, the method makes use of one of the great wonders of childhood – the imagination. We should not neglect that powerful part of a child's life in our Biblical exploration with them.

This method encourages the children to have a workbook and to use it creatively. In this example the child is asked to imagine that he or she is on a desert island.

EXAMPLE PEOPLE WHO NEED ME

You can take three things that will be useful on your desert island. Draw them in your workbook. Then off you go to your island.

Will you write to your family while you are away or save it up to tell them when you get back?

> Read: John 3:14-15

Draw one of the adventures you had on the island. Now read about a boy coming home to his family after a long time away.

> Read: Luke 15:20

Who would be most pleased to see you when you get back?
Would they have missed you?

Draw a picture of your family without you, all looking sad.
Now draw them again with you there as well. Are they looking happier in this picture?

Think why your family needs you.

Find some more people who need you — a friend who wants to play, a boy or girl who has no one to play with, a friend in trouble, a new child in your school, your teacher.

There are many people in the world who are unhappy or ill or hungry. They need you too. They need you to pray for them. Will you help them by your prayers?

> Read: 2 Corinthians 1:11

■ SCRIPTURE AND CHILDREN IN CHURCH

The use of the Bible in our church-based instruction of children has been, and sometimes still is, a hit-and-miss affair. There is a danger that we overdo the use of Scripture with children in our Sunday Schools or periods of children's instruction. Unfortunately we sometimes tend to give children Bible stories alone and to ignore two other vital elements: first, Scripture's interaction with the real life of the children and, second, its relation to the Church's worshipping life.

It has already been stressed in this chapter that the Bible and the experiences of the child must be linked in a real and tangible way. The message of the passage will mean little if it is not seen to be relevant. The Bible flashes where it touches our real lives, however young or old we may be.

Scripture also has to be linked to the child's experience of the church. Most will grow up within a particular way of worshipping and a particular set of traditions.

They need to see, hear and feel that Scripture is important for that worshipping community, not that it is something you 'grow out of' when you get older. Unfortunately Scripture is often used as a child-minding exercise.

If it is our custom to take the children out from adult worship we must ask why we do so and what we are hoping to achieve with and for the children. Unless this is done there is a danger that we take them out and give them a Bible story because we do not know what else to do. As a result, children soon get the impression that this is not really part of the church's worship or teaching; it is nothing special and they are being occupied for a time while the adults get on with 'important things.' To make matters worse, we often do this with the poorest of equipment and resources, which can only add to the feeling that this time is a fill-in period. It is no wonder that they get the impression that the Bible is not very important.

A good many of the problems associated with withdrawing children from Sunday adult worship can be overcome by ensuring that the children see the link between what they are doing with Scripture and what the adults are doing. A link is needed between the way Scripture is handled, used and approached by the adults, and the way it is handled, used and approached with the children. Obviously the methods will be different but the reverence for Scripture, the link between Scripture and worship and its importance for living should be made clear both to adults and to children. In this respect a proper children's Liturgy of the Word can be enormously helpful. It encourages the children to use at least one of the same Scripture readings as the adults (although it will usually need shortening) and to experience a similar format for worship. In addition it enables the children to link in easily with the adults when they are old enough to stay on. It avoids the feeling that they are being taken off to be 'coped with' for the duration of the sermon, and encourages the awareness that Scripture is as important for children as it is for adults.

The Grail produce a number of Liturgies of the Word for children, from which the following material (both guidelines and example) is taken: *Liturgies of the Word*, compiled by Paddy Rylands, published by The Grail. The framework for this is based on the format of the Liturgy off the Word section of a Roman Catholic Sunday Eucharistic celebration. The example is for the 33rd Sunday in Ordinary Time, Year B.

Preparation

"One first step in preparing the Liturgy of the Word is for the planning team to meet and choose a theme. Almost without exception we base this on the readings for the day.

The next step is to decide how the chosen theme is going to be expressed through singing and quiet music, 'listening' and silent parts, through spoken parts and the active participation of the children. As with any good liturgy it is necessary to find the right balance of each of these elements. If young musicians are involved we have found it important to plan sufficiently in advance for them to be familiar enough with the hymns to be able to lead us competently. It makes a noticeable difference to the celebration when the children, whether Saturday Class or School Group, have taken part in the preparation. So, although it may mean more work for the team, this involvement is certainly to be encouraged.

Framework

The team's discussion must have covered all the items in the following simple framework:

Summary of the Theme
Visual presentation
Opening hymn
Penance Rite
Bible Procession and Prayer
Reading (possibly a psalm or hymn)
Gospel Acclamation
Gospel
Response to the Word
Homily given by the Catechist (perhaps leading to the children being asked to do something)
Creed (if included)
Bidding Prayers (usually spontaneous)
Hymn as the children process into the church to join their families at the Offertory

How it works

The children come into the hall or room set aside for them, expectantly, knowing they are coming to worship. So, it is important that this is reflected by the preparation and arrangement of the hall or room. Quiet taped music sets an atmosphere. A wall chart or brightly-coloured board reflecting the theme provides a good focal point. The table, covered with a white cloth (not creased!) on which is a vase of flowers and the empty Bible stand, reminds the children that they have come to the 'table of the Word'.

As an alternative to chairs use a carpet or carpet squares for the children to sit on. We arrange these in a semicircle round the table. As well as reducing the noise it means we don't have to worry about whether or not we have put out enough chairs because two children can sit comfortably on some of the squares.

Decide from where your Bible procession will approach. It can come from the back of the hall. Four children carry lighted candles and one carries the Bible. If you have musicians it helps them to feel important (and so play better) if they are placed in a prominent position. Two or three of the children can be asked to give out the liturgy sheets to the others as they come in. This helps to create the important feeling of being welcomed. It is good if one of the team can also be there to welcome the children by name.

If the doing bit requires pens etc. make sure these are readily available so that they can be distributed without disrupting the atmosphere of the celebration.

When the children return to the adults at the offertory the celebrant welcomes them to the Liturgy of the Eucharist. This draws the children and adults closely together."

EXAMPLE

I WILL BRING ALL MY FRIENDS TOGETHER

Opening hymn
He's got the whole world in his hand

Penance Rite
(The Penance Rite is led by one of the team who simply asks the Lord for forgiveness for the times we have spoilt our friendship with him or one another.)
Lord, have mercy. Christ, have mercy. Lord, have mercy.

Bible Procession
Let us pray:
Lord God, we have come together to praise and thank you. We have come together to listen to your Word. Help us, your people, as we get ready to listen to you. You speak in the words of your Son who is Word of God. Amen.

Reading: Psalm 15
We praise the Lord
for he guides us along the right path.
By day and by night
he shows us what to do.
We shall not fall down
if he is there beside us.
Lord we are happy
for we are safe with you.

Gospel Acclamation
Alleluia, Alleluia.
I will bring all my friends together.
They will be happy with me for ever.
Alleluia.

Gospel Reading
Today's reading is from Saint Mark's Gospel, Chapter 13, verses 24 to 32 (taken from Collins, *Listen*, p.913)

Homily
(On the theme of being one of God's friends, using the 'Jesus with his friends' picture on page 100)

Bidding Prayers

Hymn
Shalom, my friend

JESUS WITH HIS FRIENDS

Where are you?
We've left a space for you to draw yourself close to Jesus. Put it in your bedroom this week to remind you that we are Jesus' friends.

■ SCRIPTURE AND CHILDREN'S ACTIVITIES

So far we have looked at how Scripture can be used on a Sunday during worship, but a good many activities take place for children either during the week or separately on a Sunday. These may take the form of Sunday Schools, mid-week clubs or Saturday instruction classes. In the Roman Catholic tradition the vast majority of religious instruction is done in schools and by families. However, there are parishes with no schools or parishes where most parents cannot or do not send their children to a Catholic school. Here opportunities for the children must be provided at some other time and in some other way.

Scripture should be a natural and important part of such activities. Of course, there will be other things as well as Scripture stories that we want the children to discover, such as ways of praying, experiencing friendship, learning what the Church believes and what it means to trust in God. We shall want them to grow in their faith, and using the Bible will be an important element in the whole experience of living and growing in the Christian life. Here is one example of a programme used with children during Lent. There were about 20 children aged seven to nine years of age who met on a Saturday morning. The five weeks' work is given in outline and the first session is given in detail. This example is important because it shows clearly the vital relationship between Scripture, other examples in the life of the Church or world and the children's own experience. Note too that the sessions had a spiralling structure:

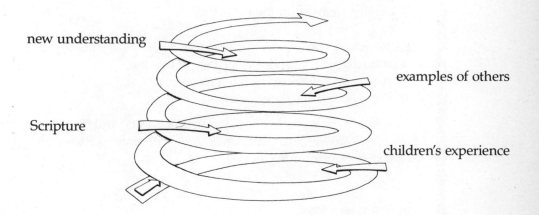

new understanding

examples of others

Scripture

children's experience

EXAMPLE   FRIENDS OF JESUS

Outline of the sessions

Aim: To help children to know that Jesus is with them in all their experiences and is their friend at all times.

Session 1: Jesus calls us to be his friends
  The call to be friends of Jesus
  The call of the disciples (Mark 1:16-20)

Session 2: Jesus is the friend of the lonely
  Jesus is with us when we are alone
  The story of Zacchaeus (Luke 19:1-10)

Session 3: Jesus is the friend of the sick
  Jesus is with us when we are ill
  Jesus comes to Peter's mother-in-law (Mark 1:29-31)

Session 4: Jesus is friend of the sad
  Jesus is with us even when we are sad
  Jesus forgives (Luke 7:36-48)

Session 5: Jesus is the friend of the happy (Palm Sunday)
    Jesus is our friend in good times
    Jesus enters Jerusalem (Luke 19:29-40)

Note: The Scripture passages were not read verbatim to the children. The story was told in each case by the leader using simple visuals.

SESSION 1: JESUS CALLS US TO BE HIS FRIENDS

The children began with a news time in which news of the week was told.

Prayer
(including items from the news time)

Children's experience
- Who are your friends? Why do you like them?
- What is good about having a friend?
- What is difficult about being a friend?

Children were asked to shout out their answers, and these were simply listed as one-word answers. (It could also be done with simple pictures either by the children or by the leader.)

Scripture experience
Jesus calls the disciples (Mark 1:16-20)
- Why do you think the disciples wanted to be Jesus' friend?

The experience of others
Mother Teresa of Calcutta was used here as the example of someone called by Jesus to be his friend and the friend of others.

Children's experience
Activity: there are endless opportunities here. It could be a drama of either the Scripture passage or a modern-day equivalent. It could be the making of a frieze (in the parish a frieze was built up each week for display in the church at Easter). It could be the making of a Friends of Jesus Book, one for each child. In all cases an explicit link must be made between the theme and what the children will do during the week.
- How will we try to be better friends of Jesus and friends of others?
- What does Jesus want us to do this week for other people?

Closing prayer and song
Lord Jesus, we are glad to be your friends. Help us to remember you are with us always. Amen.

(This prayer was used each week.)

■ SCRIPTURE AND HOLIDAY CLUBS

A growing number of local churches are concerned to do something for children during the long holiday periods, especially in the summer. The children are bored, parents are at their wits' end and the church itself is often not doing much during these summer months. Running a week of activities for children during this period is not easy. It takes preparation, planning and resources but it is a glorious opportunity for the church to help not only their own children but others in the neighbourhood.

The use of the Bible in such a week must be handled with the utmost care. Many of the children may not be associated with the church or have much awareness of what it is all about. The week may be a means of communication with such families but it should not be designed to 'get the Bible over because they will not get it in any other way'. Such an attitude and heavy-handedness are likely to ensure they will never return! How, then, can such a week be organised and run so that the Bible has a central part, but one which is not intrusive?

Here is how the Christians in one small town undertook a week of activities from planning to follow-up. The week was an ecumenical event and involved both adults and children from all the main denominations (and none!) in the town.

EXAMPLE

SEARCH '84

Planning

The planning group formed from all churches met to discuss six main questions:

1. Do we have sufficient support from our churches for the work we hope to do this week?

2. Do we have a sufficient number of people with the right skills to staff the week?

3. Do we have the right facilities and enough resources?

4. What is our aim for the week? What are we trying to do?

5. What will be our theme for the week?

6. What should be the balance between games, activities, Biblical work, stories and outings each day?

The group made the following decisions:

● The group chose as their theme 'Those who help us'.
● The aim was to show children that discovering what we believe could be fun as well as instructive.
● Each day was to begin at 9.30am and end at 4pm. Children could either go home for lunch or bring sandwiches.
● The week was to be held in a church hall which had a good number of rooms as well as the main hall.
● Resources in the way of equipment for games, activity material such as paints,

paper, old magazines, cardboard boxes for models, glue etc. was to be provided by the local church members. This had the added advantage of involving more people in supporting the event.

- The event was made known through the participating churches and schools.
- A very small charge was to be made (15p a day).
- Arrangements were to be made to ensure that the event was adequately insured.
- There were to be three (half-day) outings during the week.
- More adults were to be recruited than might be needed!
- There were to be some simple but clear rules for the children, the breaking of which incurred immediate expulsion. (These were largely for safety's sake — e.g. no sliding down the bannisters!)
- The daily programme would include activities, games, Bible work, story and music.
- The whole event was to be a 'fun' activity. The week was a holiday activity and not to be confused with school!
- The week was for children aged seven to twelve.

The daily plan

The daily programme was the same each day:

09.15   Arrival. (Children were usually given something to do immediately or a game was in progress in which they could join.)

09.45   Introduction to the day's theme. The children were divided into two age groups, seven to nine and ten to twelve. (This time was aimed at drawing out from the children their own experience of the theme.) There followed a look at a modern-day helper – usually an organisation or agency.

10.00   Activity time – on the theme (usually art and craft, some drama, making models etc.). (During this time drinks were provided.)

11.00   Games. (Children were given a colour when they arrived and there was a large team chart for scoring.)

12.00   Lunch. (Most went home.)

13.00   Scripture time – an exploration of a Scripture passage linking the theme of the day with activities.

13.45   Outings (on second, third and fourth days). Open afternoon for parents and friends showing the work of the week on the last afternoon.

16.00   Depart.

The plan of the week

Monday — People who help us when we are in trouble
What sort of trouble do we find ourselves in?
How do we feel?
Exploration of the Life Boat Service
Scripture: Jesus and the storm at sea

Tuesday — People who help us when we are sick
What is it like to be ill?
Who helps us?
Doctors and Nurses (a visit by a local GP was arranged)
Scripture: Jesus helps the sick
Outing: the Medical Centre

Wednesday — People who help us when we lose the way
In what ways do we get lost?
The Police Service
Scripture: Jesus our leader (following Jesus as his friend)
Outing: the local Police Station

Thursday — People who help us when we are trapped
Have you ever been trapped?
What is it like to be shut in?
Scripture: Jesus 'rescues' blind Bartimaeus
Outing: the Fire Station

Friday — People who help us at home
Who are the people who help us?
Families, friends? How do they help?
Scripture: Jesus goes to a party (the wedding at Cana)
Afternoon: open to parents — closing party

Notes
1. The week exhausts everyone! This particular week had 120 children.
2. There needs to be a good number of adults for each session. A rota system can be devised but there must be some able to come every day for the sake of continuity.
3. Arrangements for the outings need to be made early.
4. The hall should be available all week so that tables, art work etc. can be left lying around. It adds to the already heavy work-load if it has to be cleared up each evening!
5. The Scriptural element needs to be seen as an important part of the day but it should not be overdone.

Scripture and Young People

'You just don't understand!' he shouted, slamming the door and storming out of the house. They never understood; at least, that is what John felt. He wandered down the street, angrily kicking a tin can. Why were older people always so blind? Why couldn't they see? He was clear about it all. Yet with the possible exception of his grandmother there seemed to be a wall between him and the other adults in his life. He would not be like that when he was older. He would understand. He wouldn't get himself into the sort of rut it seemed to him that his parents were in. He wouldn't get set in his ways or be content to live for ever with compromises. He would let his children decide for themselves what to believe; he wouldn't mind them 'rebelling' — not that he really thought of himself as a rebel. He simply wanted to explore new ideas and to test them against his own experience. If there was anything in this faith business he wanted it to be real and his, not just the handed-down faith of his parents.

All the feelings described above cannot be ignored when we come to consider using the Bible with young people. There is a danger that we ignore these powerful emotions or consider them unimportant. Like John's parents we can feel that they are just 'being awkward'. In fact, working with young people and Scripture can be very stimulating because they bring to the Bible a freshness and clarity which we who are older often fail to see.

Basic principles

1. When we consider how to work with young people and how to help them discover the richness of Scripture the most important point to remember is not one of methods but one of attitudes. During the course of many years in many parishes I have seen a good number of attempts at youth work, the vast majority of which have run into problems of one sort or another. I suspect that one of the reasons for this is that we adults fail lamentably to enter into the minds of young people. We have forgotten what it was like to be young; to be going through that stage of questioning; that period of testing out our own stories against those of others. We have forgotten the confusion of growing up and the conflicting emotions of needing to be independent and yet needing security. We have forgotten how it felt to be sure of everything, of what was right and wrong, of how everything was seen in terms of bright colours and there were no areas of grey. This need to enter into the attitudes of young people, to feel with them and experience with them their certainties and uncertainties, is essential for any use of Scripture with them.

2. We need to remember that young people want and need to test the story they have been brought up with against other stories. They will question — sometimes illogically. They will try out new theories and new ideas. The worst attitude to have where Scripture is concerned is to be defensive. Young people want to explore the truths of the Bible. They will not be convinced by a rigid fundamentalism, but neither will they be happy if they feel there is a 'watering down' going on. They require an honest answer to an honest question and an explanation which seems to them to be tenable.

3. Work with the Bible needs to be subject-oriented. In other words we need to start with the young people's real-life experiences and show the relevance of the Bible to them. Very few young people are interested in Biblical study for its own sake. Most want to test out its message against their own experience. Does what it says about God ring true?

4. Work with the Bible also needs to be attractive. This applies to any age but, in particular, young people need to experience a variety of ways of discovering the riches of the Word of God. Drama, music, cassettes and 'doing' are all important.

5. Work with the Bible should be fun! It should be aimed at clarification. This is not the time to present the complexities of Biblical scholarship! Instead, exploring Scripture should be characterised by a certain simplicity of approach. Remember that simplicity is NOT the same as simpleness, much less simple-mindedness!

★   ★   ★

These principles can be seen in the two examples that follow. The first is designed for use in a small group, while the second uses role playing as a means of exploring a Biblical passage.

EXAMPLE 1   ## STORMY WEATHER

After the group has assembled have a time for general chat (perhaps over coffee).

Step 1   Divide the group into small groups (no more than four in a group).

Step 2   ● Ask one group to discuss any situation in their own lives which they would describe as a 'sunny' experience.
● Ask another to discuss any situation in their own lives which they would describe as 'grey and overcast'.
● Ask another to discuss any situation in their own lives which they would describe as 'blizzard conditions'.
(If you have more than three groups repeat the process with the others.) The small groups may suggest something they all have in common or pick a particular experience of one member.

Step 3   Share these experiences in the whole group. Describe how you felt – great, bored, scared etc.

Step 4   Read the text (Mark 9:2-8):

And after six days Jesus took with him Peter and James and John, and led them up a high mountain apart by themselves; and he was transfigured before them, and his garments became glistening, intensely white as no fuller on earth could bleach them. And there appeared to them Elijah with Moses; and they were talking to Jesus. And Peter said to Jesus, 'Master, it is well that we are here; let us make three booths, one for you and one for Moses and one for Elijah.' For he did not know what to say, for they were exceedingly afraid. And a cloud overshadowed them, and a voice came out of the cloud, 'This is my beloved Son; listen to him.' And suddenly looking around they no longer saw anyone with them but Jesus only.

Discuss if you would describe this passage as 'sunny', 'grey and overcast' or a 'blizzard'!

Step 5 With a tape recorder choose an interviewer, and three people as the disciples. You can also have other people, such as those who heard the story at second hand. Interview the disciples as to how they felt, what happened. Interview the crowd; do you believe it? What do they think happened etc?

Step 6 Reflection
Ask participants to think for a moment in silence about how they would react if they came face to face with Jesus. Would they:
● be so scared they would run a mile?
● be so astounded they would fall on their faces?
● be so stunned they would be unable to move?
● be so curious they would go closer to investigate?
● other reactions.

Close with a prayer or song.

EXAMPLE 2   FOLLOWERS OF THE WAY

This method uses drama but in a very lighthearted and unrehearsed way.

Step 1 Divide the group into pairs (or larger groups if you have a big number). You need six groups or pairs.

Step 2 Ask each pair to be a particular disciple. Give each a list of the appropriate references and ask them to work out a 'character study' of the disciple. What sort of person? What sort of personality? What reactions to Jesus?

Peter:	Mark 8:27-33; Luke 22:31-34; John 18:25-27; 21:1-17
Philip:	John 1:43-46; 14:8-10
Thomas:	John 14:5; 20:24-29
Matthew:	Luke 5:27-32
James and John:	Mark 1:19-20; 10:35-45
Judas:	John 12:1-8; Matthew 27:1-5; Luke 22:47-48

Step 3 When all have finished act out the following:

- Each disciple introduces himself/herself, giving a bit of background.
- Other disciples react and ask questions. (Can't see me going around with a tax collector! What's it like being a twin? Thomas, do you ever believe anything anyone tells you? etc.)
- 'Act out' what you can't stand about each other; what you like about each other.

Allow the role playing to go on as long as is comfortable.

Step 4 Discuss what you have discovered about the relationships between the disciples in the Gospels.

- What has this to say about our following of Jesus?
- What does it have to say about our relationships with other people in the Church?

Notes

1. The leader may have to do a bit of prompting to get the role play going.
2. It is important to 'de-role' the participants.
3. Our discoveries about the followers in the Gospels must be related to how we follow Jesus today and how we do this with others; how we cope with others; how all sorts of people with different ideas and personalities are equally important to God.

Chapter 6

SPECIAL EVENTS AND SCRIPTURE

THERE ARE special times in the lives of most local churches, particular moments of importance or celebration. These may range from jubilee celebrations or art and craft fairs to flower festivals or exhibitions. In most churches too there are events which happen occasionally, such as Days of Recollection or Quiet, special concerts, drama events or parish days. These special moments are not usually connected with Scripture in any overt way, and in many cases there is no reason why they should be. We should not be concerned to drag the Bible into every parish event! However, sometimes the Scriptures can come to life in a very natural way within such special events.

Basic principles

Before we look at the role of the Bible in these special moments in the life of a parish we need to bear one or two important points in mind.

● This chapter is dealing with events which are not 'normal' parish events. They are particular and special and that means that most of them will require a considerable amount of time and thought before the event actually happens. This preparation is as important as the event itself. Depending on the type of activity the church is planning it is sometimes possible to include a look at the Word of God during this preparation period; indeed, it will sometimes be vitally important to do so.

● There are often 'spin-offs' to these special events. It is important that the church makes the most of its opportunities. Sometimes a greater awareness of the need to understand and meet God in the Scriptures comes through some particular happening in the church. This is especially true of events such as Bible Days or Bible Weeks. So there needs to be some forward planning for what may happen *after* the event.

● Some special events are obviously *not* the vehicle for present or future work with the Scriptures.

We must be careful not to force the Bible into every situation. It might be that a parish holding a concert to raise funds for the organ might start or finish the evening with a short Scriptural prayer or reading, but to try to do anything else would be more likely to put people off the Bible rather than attract them.

Let us look, then, at five special events a parish might hold at sometime. Three of them are specifically Biblical and come in Section 2; that is, they are designed to help people understand the Scriptures or to give them a greater love of them. Two are the events which might contain work with Scripture in a very natural way, while not being in themselves specifically Scriptural activities. These come in Section 1. There are undoubtedly other special events in the life of any parish in addition to these, the basic principles and ideas presented here could be used at these other special times too.

SECTION 1

Parish days and festivals

Many local churches have discovered the value of occasionally getting people together for a day. However, one of the difficulties has been encouraging as many people as possible to attend. It is asking a good deal of people to give up a precious day off, especially if they have families. Yet such an event can help people to discover a fresh sense of purpose and fellowship that cannot be gained in literally a month of Sundays. Whole families can take part and people can get a chance to get to know each other better. It can also be a wonderful opportunity of opening up the Scriptures in a very practical way. However, there are, admittedly, many difficulties involved. Family Days, Away Days, Parish Days – call them what you will – do not run themselves, and it is essential to think through exactly what the aim of the day is to be and to prepare carefully for it. Here is an example of what *NOT* to do!

> The first the parish heard about it was an announcement on Sunday morning. Everyone settled themselves as comfortably as possible into their seats, and then the priest launched into a list of forthcoming events, dates and places which they needed to remember.
>
> 'Then on Saturday week,' he said, 'we shall be having a Parish Day. It will be held in the parish hall and is open to everyone of any age. Do please come along.'
>
> In fact, the whole day turned out to be a disaster. Most of the Parish Council, who had had the date in their diaries for weeks, were there. They felt that, as they had agreed to the event, they ought to be there, and a few other stalwarts turned up. They got off to a rather late start because Mrs Mellor, the hall caretaker, had forgotten they were coming. Consequently they decided to dispense with the planned opening worship and get down to the business in hand. The priest gave a rather long talk which those who knew him well soon realised they had heard several times before. The children seemed at a loss and it was only after the talk that they went off to play. The teenagers were bored stiff with all the talk and didn't want to be there anyway. The adults went off into groups but were unsure exactly what they were supposed to be discussing. Everyone went home for lunch and, it has to be admitted, a good number did not come back. Those who did continued their discussions in the afternoon and the day fizzled out with a cup of tea at about 4.30 pm, although many people rushed off to catch the shops before they closed. The priest was disappointed and felt he had not been supported. His colleague in the next parish, St Mary's, had enthused at how helpful a Parish Day had been in his parish and how much people had got out of it, but somehow it just didn't seem to work at St Johns.

The priest at St Mary's was right, of course. These Parish Days can be of immense value to a parish. They can also be useful in helping people in their handling and understanding of Scripture. But they must be planned well and there must be a specific aim.

■ PLANNING

When planning such a day the following points need to be borne in mind:

1. The reason for holding such an event needs to be discussed thoroughly. What is the purpose of such a day? What is to be the theme? It is all too easy to get lost in generalities and to try to do too much all at once.

2. If such a day is going to take place it will also require some sort of planning group to ensure that everyone knows who is doing what and what facilities there will be for children and young people.

3. The group will have to consider who the day is aimed at. Is it for a specific group within the parish (e.g. all parents who have had children baptised in the parish during the last year) or is it for everyone in the parish?

4. There will need to be some thought about whether the day is going to be a do-it-yourself event, using only the resources which lie within the parish, or whether someone from outside is to be invited to take part. If such a person is to be invited then it is vital that early contact is made and continued throughout the planning. There is nothing so likely to court disaster as a parish coming with one set of expectations and the invited resource person coming with another.

This is particularly important where Scripture is concerned. If someone is to be invited they must know exactly what is expected of them. Do the parish want some sort of Bible Study, do they want some experiences of how to handle the Bible, do they want practical help in using it or do they want some direct input of a more academic kind? If this is not sorted out very early people are likely to be disappointed.

5. The planning group will also have to decide where this event is to take place. Is it to be within the parish or is this to be a chance for the community to move to a different setting for the day? There are advantages to both. Staying at home has the advantage of familiarity and closeness and probably cost. Going away has the advantage of fresh stimulation and a new atmosphere. It will also mean that people are less likely to fall prey to the temptation to nip back home during the day!

6. The day, of course, must be booked well in advance and plenty of notice given to everyone. When considering the date the group will need to see if there are likely to be any other 'rival' attractions (e.g. F.A. Cup Final day is not a good choice). The event should be publicised well in a very positive way.

7. The very practical side of the day must be considered. If it is to be for all the parish, including the children, what arrangements are to be made for them? Who is going to do the catering? Are people going to be asked to bring a packed lunch or is something to be provided? Is there anything else they need to bring: pen and pencil? Bible? etc. What time is the day to start? It is vital that starting and finishing times are set and adhered to. People need to know that they will be away on time.

8. What exactly is to be the content of the day? What will be the timetable? It is vital that the day's activities, like all group work whether large or small, have the elements of variety and creativity we mentioned in Chapter 3. The day should not consist of small discussion groups and nothing else! Nor should people go away feeling that they have spent the whole day being talked *at*. What joint activities will

there be for the children and adults together? What percentage of time will be given to input, and what to sharing in smaller groups or to individual reflection?

9. The planning group must also think about how the worship is to be arranged. It is a must for most Parish Days. What sort of worship is it to be? Who will do it? How will all the groups (including the children) be involved? How is the theme to be reflected in the worship? Will it take place at the beginning or the end of the day?

10. Finally, the group will have to consider what follow-up to the day is likely to be required. This applies both to the participants and to those who were unable to come. Those who were not present must know what happened and not feel 'left out'. Those who did come need to see the day as part of an on-going process and not just a one-off event.

Here is an example of how one church planned and ran a Parish Day on the theme of 'Exploring our Gifts'. It was a day for all the parish and had separate activities for children, young people and adults. However, the worship included everyone. It was held within the parish using parish resources, with no 'experts' present.

■ THE PARISH DAY

EXAMPLE

Preparation

The idea for the day arose from the parish situation. There was a great deal going on, with a good number of organisations and activities happening throughout the parish. The difficulty experienced by the church was that many people were not involved at all and that those who were involved often failed to comm9unciate with one another. A need was felt to come together and explore what it meant to be a member of this particular church today. Since many people would not come out in the evenings, and it was difficult to arrange a date that did not clash with some groups or other, a Saturday was planned. A small group of five people became the planning group and they began their deliberations four months before the proposed date. They liaised with the organisations in the parish, thrashed out the theme and the programme, and saw to all the practical arrangements.

The Day

When the day came it was held in the local primary school which had plenty of rooms for group work and for children to have their own activities. It also had the advantage of having plenty of equipment.

Participants began to arrive at about 10.00 for coffee and the first item on the agenda for the day was due to start at 10.30. As this day was open to anyone in the parish it was important to ensure that there was time for people to chat and settle in. However, to prevent the children running riot and any feeling of 'hanging around' on the part of the adults, each family or individual was given a task: they were to draw on a sheet of paper their own made-up family crest showing the talents or gifts of each family member. Those who had come alone, or who had no immediate family, were asked to do the same including their own gift and that of their closest friends. These were put up around the hall.

When everyone had assembled there was a short liturgy. It consisted of a hymn, a short reading from 1 Cor 12:4-11, and a prayer. The children then went off to their own sessions. They were to look in the morning at 'helping each other' (the whole idea of using our talents to help others). One of their major tasks was to make a huge frieze on the theme, to be used as a focal point for the Eucharist at the end of the day.

The adults and young people then looked together at what it means to be an active member of the church. This was done through the presentation of a 'drama' (with two leaders drawing in the rest of the group). This presentation was based on the life of the early church as recorded in Acts 2:42-47. It involved all those present and showed clearly that all are called to play an active part in the ministry of the church and to use the talents they have been given. The material used was taken from the first part of *The Way We Were* by Michael Fewell (T. Shand Publications, 1985).

Participants were split into small groups (the young people having their own) to discuss the following:

(a) Share your immediate reactions to what you have just seen, heard and experienced.
(b) The Church seen in Acts shows a whole community working together. What does this say about our own community?
(c) Share one experience in your life when you have felt God working through another person. What did that person do or say? What attitudes did he or she show?

Lunch consisted of a shared table. Tea and coffee was provided but people brought a packed lunch and this was put together and a buffet meal prepared from it. The lunch time was deliberately kept reasonably short to make sure that there was no dropping off of enthusiasm!

In the afternoon the children again went off. They played games and carried on their other activities, which included the making of their own family talent book to be taken home.

The young people spent most of the afternoon working out a drama for presentation at the Eucharist based on the Parable of the Talents. The adults looked at how the local church should be using the talents of its members. To do this they first undertook a short exercise to discover their own gifts. This consisted of asking each person to write down what they saw as their own gift or talent, which included practical skills. These pieces of paper were collected and a master list drawn up. Next they used the 'drawing our lives' exercise outlined in Chapter 3 (pp. 42–43), in the same small groups in which they had been during the morning.

The drawing caused a considerable amount of amusement, but it did result in bringing out many feelings that people would have been unwilling to put into words. These pictures were done on large sheets of paper and put around the walls, and time was allowed for everyone to look at them. Following this, there was a short 'input' on what the Church teaches about the role of the laity and their task in the world of today.

Finally the adults in small groups looked at the following questions:

1. What talents and gifts do we have amongst us that we did not know about before?

2. How are the talents of people being used?

3. What do our drawings tell us about our church now? What do they tell us about what we should be doing?

All the small groups came back together, having been asked to write down their findings on large sheets of paper. These were displayed and *one* decision of a practical nature for the future was made.

The day came to an end with a Eucharist at which the day's work was summed up and celebrated. The readings were from Ephesians 4:11-13 and Matthew 25:14-30. All were involved in this informal (and noisy!) celebration. The children produced their frieze at the beginning with the celebrant undertaking a question-and-answer explanation of what was on it; the young people did their drama of the Parable of the Talents during the reading of the Gospel and pieces of paper on which the adults had written their own gifts were brought up at the Offertory.

Tea was served before everyone returned home. The day ended at 4.00 pm.

The Follow-up

The original planning group met during the week following the Parish Day to consider what follow-up was required. This consisted of a special handout to be given to every parishioner on the following Sunday telling them what had happened and an article for the parish magazine. They had also ensured that someone with a camera had been around during the day, and planned a display for the back of the church. In this way anyone who had been unable to be at the day would not feel left out. They then turned to future planning. As a result of the day the parish has decided that they will try to make more use of the artistic talent that revealed itself during the day and to plan a short series of sessions on 'listening skills' for the many people in the parish involved in pastoral care.

This type of day could be used with a purely Scriptural theme, and this has been done very successfully. However, note that in this example the use of Scripture was paramount, although not the major theme. It was used as a natural focus for the consideration of the parish in its planning for the future. Using Scripture in this way also helped people to see its importance and relevance for their life in the Church today.

A day such as this should not be held too often. Part of its value is that it is a special event and, as such, has a particular appeal that could be lost if it became routine.

■ THE PARISH FESTIVAL

Festivals of one sort or another are not uncommon in the life of many churches. Flower festivals, harvest festivals, music festivals and occasionally community festivals are now part of our church life. These special events during the year are times of celebration, and celebrations of one sort or another are a common theme within Scripture. As with Parish Days we must be careful not to drag Scripture into these events by the back door; however, the sensible use of Scripture within a parish festival can provide a chance for the community to experience the richness and power of the Word of God. This is easy to see for events such as harvest festivals but there are other occasions which are equally suitable. Wonderful flower or music festivals can be centred around a Scriptural theme. I have seen one parish organise a whole week's festival around one psalm (in this case Psalm 104) and involve not only their own people but the wider community. Local non-church organisations such as the local photographic club and art group took the psalm and were asked to provide a display of their interpretation of it. The church was a mass of flowers, photographs, sculpture and art, while the local music groups provided three nights of concerts, all around the same theme. The whole week culminated in the harvest celebration.

An event such as the one described above takes a huge amount of time and organisation. It was nine months in the planning, but a good deal can be done on a much smaller scale. Our congregations contain some very talented people who are often involved in a range of hobbies or activities which are rarely seen by the parish community, and yet which play an extremely important part in the these people's lives. Occasionally the parish puts some of these talents to use. A parishioner who enjoys working in wood may find an opening to make a piece of church furniture, or those who can knit, sew or bake will find their contributions gratefully received by the organisers of the summer fair.

But on the whole the creative talents of many people go unnoticed or unused. Openly celebrating these God-given gifts can give people an opportunity to thank God for them and rejoice in them. Here is one example of a parish doing just that, and at the same time using a specific Scriptural theme on which to centre their celebration.

EXAMPLE   'GO AND DO LIKEWISE'

The parish chose as their theme a very well-known Biblical passage, the story of the Good Samaritan. Such a well-known parable was deliberately chosen; the parish wanted to explore it in new ways and to try to see it in a new light.

Planning began a couple of months before the proposed event. The general idea was to have a fairly low-key but meaningful celebration of the creative talent within the parish. Since there were people in the church who enjoyed various arts and crafts the weekend activity was something of an experiment in a new form of Bible exploration. It was also an experiment in community building. Those who did not feel it was 'their scene' soon found themselves drawn in, sometimes in very simple but necessary ways, such as in being asked to distribute leaflets or to provide various items ranging from tablecloths to a first-aid kit for one of the displays!

The actual event centred around a display in the church. This was on the theme of the Good Samaritan today and consisted of a surprisingly wide range of pictures, photographs, flower displays and sculpture. People were approached both individually and through the usual parish communication system of notices, bulletins and magazine. Some groups, including the school, the youth group, the scouts and guides, were also asked to participate. People brought in their contribution (there was a maximum size!) by 10.00 a.m. on the Saturday morning, and the rest of the day was spent assembling all the material and creating a display from it. The result surprised everyone and demonstrated to many people how widely the story Jesus told could be interpreted. The church was open all Saturday evening for people to come and look around, and tea and coffee were available in the parish hall.

The major celebration took place during the late afternoon on the Sunday. This was timed deliberately to give people a chance to recover from Sunday lunch but early enough not to interrupt the evening. The celebration took the form of music, readings and drama, all centred around the same theme and involving a good cross-section of people. This had been very carefully planned by a small group who studied the Word together and worked out a plan for the worship.

As in many similar events the parish discovered a considerable spin-off effect. Not only had it enabled the congregation to express the creativity that lay amongst them, but it was also a real exercise in doing things together. One of the discoveries the parish made was that people tend to work together when there is a specific aim. Working towards the celebration weekend gave a focus for their activity, a lesson from which they learnt a good deal. After the weekend the parish restructured a good deal of their activity in other areas. They learnt that it was important to set realistic targets for their work, and that people need to feel they have accomplished a task and accomplished it well. Finally they discovered that the Bible could be explored in ways which they had not dreamed possible and that the Word of God could be heard in new and exciting ways.

The above example celebrated the talents which people were already aware they had. It is also possible to run a similar activity helping people to discover talents they did not realise they had. Again this can be centred around a Biblical theme and involve local people. Workshops allowing people to explore different activities can be very successful. One local church did this on a very small scale by having four sessions, two afternoon and two evening, to which people could drop in. These were wood carving, calligraphy, art and collage. Some people started out being interested, but many just called in to see what it was all about and ended up getting very involved themselves. In this case there was no major celebration in church on the Sunday, but the results of the workshops were on display before people took their creations home with them.

SECTION 2

Special Biblical Events

Having looked at special events in the parish which are not specifically Biblical in their nature we now turn to consider special Bible activities in the parish. We can divide these into three major categories:

1. Biblical Retreats and Days;   **2.** Bible Weeks;   **3.** Bible Exhibitions.

All three can be very helpful in encouraging people to open their Bibles and to understand what the Scriptures are for. They can also help people to increase their understanding of the content of the Bible. However, these events are very definitely 'one-off' and should not be held too frequently. This applies especially to Bible Weeks and Exhibitions. Biblical Retreats can be held more frequently but even then it is important not to overdo it. In many cases churches have found it useful to join together for these events. Bible Exhibitions and Weeks can be much more effective if they cover a wider area than just one parish, and because they take a good deal of organising it is good to share this. This section will give examples of all three special events, together with some indication of their value for the local church.

■ BIBLICAL RETREATS AND DAYS

One of the saddest remarks I hear in my travels is that too often the Church does not really help people to develop a relevant spirituality. As one person told me 'The Church has taught us prayers, it has not taught us to pray'. Quite rightly, we hear a great deal about the role of the Christian community in social action of one sort or another. We are also beginning to hear the voices of many people who are expressing the need for help in the whole area of meditation and prayer. This is not new, but I suspect that it is being voiced in stronger terms now than it was even ten years ago. As I see it the need is for a meaningful form of lay spirituality that will enable people to make sense of their faith and their world. There are a number of reasons for this which might be useful to explore before we consider the role of the Bible in helping people to develop a spirituality which they feel they can make their own.

Need for calm

We live in an extremely busy and noisy world. For many people there is a longing, not to escape from it, but to find space within it when they can, as it were, recharge their batteries. People long for a little quiet and a little time to think or just to be. I have found that if people are offered opportunities which allow them to experience this space they readily accept them. Such times need not be simply an escape from a busy life (though for a short time that in itself might not be a bad thing); rather they can give to people a new strength and perspective on their daily living. It has also been my experience that many people do not want to be talked at during this time. Giving them an exhortation of how to live the Christian life or a dose of doctrine is not what most people are really looking for at such a time. They long for a chance to think for themselves and to be given time and opportunity to do so: to be fed, but to be fed in such a way that they can reflect on their faith and what it means to them. They long for a chance to explore and develop their own unique spirituality and to be given the affirmation and assurance that their own personal journey in faith is legitimate and valuable.

This expressed longing for a spirituality which 'clicks' with them might also be influenced by the society in which we live; indeed it would be surprising if this were not so. We live in a throwaway world these days. There is a real sense of impermanence and continual change which, for many people, makes the need for a spiritual base from which to operate all the more critical.

> We live in a world which is shot through with a sense of impermanence. It is an instant and throwaway world. These days we expect to be able to switch on the television and see world events, often within minutes of them happening. We have become used to obtaining most of our daily needs ready for consumption. Most of our entertainment comes to us ready made rather than home grown. We progress from one thing to another in quick succession. Everything changes: and, though it may not be in our conscious mind, the threat of a nuclear holocaust is there too. 'We might not be here tomorrow and if we are it will all be different', leads many people to an unwillingness to be committed to anything at all. Lacking a sense of stability, feeling that there is nothing solid to hold on to, many people drift and feel at the mercy of the latest wind of change. (Monica Comerford and Christine Dodd, *Many Ministries*, CTS, 1982.)

It is, I suspect, this sense of impermanence that has increased many people's awareness of the need for a spirituality which gives meaning to the everyday facts of life.

Value of Scripture

I believe the Scriptures can be of real value in this area. They offer a means of meditating on our past and on the relevance of the Word of God for today. They offer a focus around which we can think and pray, and above all they offer to us a living Word which can provide us with strength and guidance. We shall look in more detail at how Scripture can be used profitably by individuals in another chapter, but for many a communal experience of using Scripture in their spirituality can be an eye opener and a help. Biblical Retreats or Days for the parish can do just that.

These special Biblical events might be held for the whole parish or for specific groups within it; they might be just for one day or for a weekend. They might be held in the parish or some other venue which is conducive to prayer and meditation. It is important that whether it is to be for one day or for a weekend people are aware that the event is not a conference or a discussion forum. It is primarily a spiritual activity, though hopefully increased awareness of the social implications will result.

Essential elements

Here is one example of a Scripture Day held by a parish towards the end of Lent which concentrated on the theme of the Passion of Christ. Notice that in this example there are four main elements, which are necessary in any event of this kind.

1. *The venue needs to be right*. A tatty church hall with the remnants of last week's jumble sale does not help create an atmosphere for prayer! It is true, of course, that we can engage in prayer anywhere but it must also be admitted that atmosphere is important. Indeed, the environment in which an event such as this takes place is more important than we usually admit. We are inclined to dismiss the place as of little importance. In reality the atmosphere can make or break a day such as this. If you are reduced to using premises which are far from ideal there is a great deal that can be done to improve the situation. Meet in the right size room, not too big, not too small. Have it as tidy as possible (put the jumble elsewhere if possible or at least cover it up). Have a few flowers around, a few posters on the walls. With a little imagination and ingenuity a great deal can be done to ensure that the atmosphere is as conducive as possible.

2. *The day or weekend will need a good leader or resource person*. We are not asking people here to share their own ignorance. Rather there needs to be good and sensitive leadership with the right balance of input, material for thought and time to be. Such a person need not be an expert in Biblical scholarship, but he or she does need to be able to be comfortable with the text and to have prayed and studied it themselves.

3. *There must be enough silence during the day or weekend*. This will vary from group to group but a sensitive leader should be able to judge how much or how little the group requires. For this to happen there must also be enough space for people to retire to so that they can be alone. Preferably people should be able to get away and still have some sort of quiet place to go to. It is for this reason that many people have found that Diocesan Conference Centres or Pastoral Centres provide a suitable venue. Some schools, too, provide good premises. In the example given the parish went away to a centre for the day (10.00 a.m. to 4.00 p.m.).

An event for children was held in the parish during the day to give couples a chance to get away together.

4. *The Scriptural element may take the form of looking at a particular passage or looking at a specific theme*. There are advantages in both these approaches. Taking a passage enables people to become deeply immersed in one text and to draw as much as possible from it. Taking a theme and tracing it through Scripture can be an eye opener as to the range and depth of the theme and of its development. In this case the parish took a specific passage.

EXAMPLE   'BEHOLD THE MAN'

The text chosen for the day was John 18 and 19.

The day began with coffee; lunch was provided by the centre and the day ended at 4.00 p.m. with tea.

10.00   *Arrival and coffee.*
People also had a chance to discover the layout of the centre, the Chapel, sitting rooms, toilets etc.

10.30   *Session One – Maundy Thursday* (John 18:1-27)
This session looked carefully at the Gethsemane story, the Arrest and Peter's Denial. The input lasted about 30 minutes. Participants were left with a series of questions on which to meditate if they so desired. It was stressed that these 'aids to meditation' were to be used *only* if they were found helpful.
After the input people were left free to go off and 'do their own thing' until 11.45 when they reassembled.

11.45   *Session Two – Jesus and Pilate* (John 18:28 – 19:16)
This input looked at the conversation between Pilate and Jesus and the reaction of the crowd. It lasted about 20 minutes and again people were allowed to go off alone. This time they were given a short meditation based on the passage.

13.00   **Lunch**

13.45   *Session Three – The Crucifixion and Burial* (John 19:17-42)
This final input session lasted for about 30 minutes. At the end of this period people were encouraged to use their own imagination in the period of silence. Each was given an exercise which was designed to help them. They were asked:
● to picture the scene, the noise, the smell, the reactions;
● to remember what Jesus allowed others to do to him;
● to imagine what he might say to you;
● to pray about what you have discovered about yourself, God and others.
(The exercise itself contained these four parts in an expanded form.)

15.00   **Eucharist**
The Old Testament Reading was Isaiah 53:1-6
The New Testament Reading was Hebrews 4:14-16
The Gospel was John 19:1-11
The whole Eucharistic celebration was centred around the Passion and summed up the work of the day.

15.45   **Tea and Depart**

■ BIBLE WEEKS

The planning and organisation of a Bible Week is a major undertaking. Unless the parish is extremely large or active it is probably too much to consider doing the week alone. Even if members of the local church feel they could undertake the event it is still better to think on a wider scale. A Bible Week is a glorious opportunity for cooperative effort and ecumenical endeavour. It is something we can and should do together.

Objectives

The idea behind a Bible Week is to open up the world of the Bible to as wide a cross section of people as possible. The objectives of the week must be clearly set out before any actual planning is done. Generally speaking these objectives come under four main headings:

1. *To enable easy access to the Bible itself.* This means helping people to have physical access to the Word of God. In this country we are very fortunate in that Bibles are widely available. There is a whole range of translations to choose from and a huge variety of material to accompany the Scriptures. However, access to the Bible entails more than just walking into a bookshop and buying a copy. Firstly, there are some people who feel uncomfortable with books; people who find it difficult to read or who feel, rightly or wrongly, that the Bible is just too difficult to tackle. Such people would say they prefer to read the Scriptures in a more 'manageable' form. This is by no means impossible. Single Gospels can be obtained relatively cheaply, pamphlets or leaflets of passages of Scripture can also be easily obtained. These shorter passages can help bridge the gap. Secondly, some people find that in the beginning, the Scriptures are opened up for them through looking or listening rather than reading. Again videos and cassettes can provide a way in. Thirdly, access to the Scriptures means enabling people to see that this is something for them. A Bible Week must give people access to understanding what the Scriptures are and what they are for.

2. *To close the gap between the world of the Biblical scholar and the world of the Christian in the pew.* Unfortunately, a chasm seems to have opened up between the work of Biblical scholars and the ordinary man or woman who faithfully worships Sunday by Sunday. No doubt there are many reasons for this but in many ways we are still suffering from the shock waves of the last century when Biblical scholarship first made the headlines. People are still confused and muddled, and not a few still echo the saying 'Darwin has disproved the Bible'. To many people Biblical scholarship seems to be engaged in a process of stripping away as much as possible from the Bible and 'watering down the truth'. In reality, of course, such study of the Scriptures adds to our understanding of truth, but the gap between what the scholars have discovered and are discovering and the popular interpretation of Scripture is wider than many like to admit. One of the purposes of a Bible Week is to show how Biblical scholarship can be a positive help to our hearing of the Word and that there is nothing to be afraid of in our explorations.

3. *To encourage people to see the relevance of the Scriptures for their own lives.* The week is not about uncovering the wonders of an ancient book. It is about helping people discover it as a living library.

4. *To promote regular reading of the Bible.* This will require giving people the experience of engaging with Scripture themselves. People will learn the value and relevance of the text when they engage in the actual experience of discovering it for themselves. So the week needs to have an experiential element as well as being an instrument for giving information.

★   ★   ★

It must be remembered that a Bible Week is *not* a Bible Study week. Its aim is to give an overall view of what this concern with the Bible is all about, and as such it requires a considerable amount of variety in its programme, both in presentation and in what is actually on offer.

Planning

If such a week is planned then there must be a very committed coordinating group at the centre. This will be especially important if the event is to involve several churches or denominations. Such a group may need to appoint subgroups to handle particular elements of the week. This coordinating group will need to look at exactly what the week is expected to achieve, at the contents and at all the practicalities that will have to be sorted out. This is bound to be a lengthy process, so a long planning period must be allowed. Among the questions the group will have to consider area:

- When are we planning to hold the week? Will it clash with anything else?
- What are our aims and objectives?
- What is going to be our major theme or slogan?
- Who are we aiming the week at?
- What ages are we going to cover? Are we aiming solely at adults or at other ages too?
- What outline programme can we sort out? Are we concentrating on evenings only or are there to be events during the day as well?
- What sort of celebrations are we planning? What about worship?
- What practical details need to be sorted out? (Venue, catering, car parking etc.)
- What advertising are we going to do? When and how?
- What resource people or organisations will we need to contact?

Here is the outline programme of a Bible Week undertaken by a deanery. The week ran from Sunday to Sunday. The daily events were held in a central parish and concentrated mainly on evening activities, except for the Saturday event. There was, however, a well-stocked bookstall which included posters, pictures, children's books and cassettes, as well as Bibles and books about the Bible. In addition there was a small, simple display entitled 'The Land of the Bible' which had photographs and articles from Israel. This was a do-it-yourself display mainly using pictures and souvenirs provided by church members who had been lucky enough to visit the Holy Land. The week was geared mainly to adults.

EXAMPLE

THE BOOK

Sunday	Service of worship (a Liturgy of the Word)
Monday	Film on the Land of the Bible Coffee Short talk on 'What is the Bible?'
Tuesday	'Is it true?' (questions and answers about the Bible)
Wednesday	Exploring the Bible (work in small groups on a specific text)
Thursday	Praying the Bible (an experience of using the Bible in prayer) Coffee Bible Vigil
Friday	What the children say (an exhibition of work by children of the local school) Bible Drama (aimed at adults)
Saturday	Down by the Riverside (a Deanery afternoon and picnic at a local beauty spot)
Sunday	Closing celebration

Notes

1. On the Sunday opening service a Bible was solemnly brought through the church and 'enthroned' in a place of honour where it remained throughout the week.
2. The Wednesday exploration was designed to help people experience how the Bible can be used.

■ BIBLE EXHIBITIONS

Like Bible Weeks a Bible Exhibition is aimed at introducing the Bible to as large a number of people as possible. It is designed to interest people in and to give them a taste for Scripture in the hope that they will go on to explore further.

The amount of work required for a Bible Exhibition varies, depending on the scale of the proposed undertaking. It could be a fairly small affair at the back of the church or a much larger event in a hall or school. In both cases care must be taken to make sure that the exhibition is presented well. There is nothing more calculated to put people off than an exhibition which reeks of amateurism and half-heartedness. If it is to be done it must be done well. In this connection is is probably best to aim at something small and do it as well as possible rather than to bite off too much and find it cannot be done properly.

Objectives

Any Bible Exhibition, whether large or small, must aim at fulfilling three criteria:
- *It must attract attention.* People must find it attractive and want to see what it is all about. As such, the siting of the exhibition, the colours, the design and the layout will need to be carefully thought about.
- *It must be relevant.* People must not go away thinking 'it makes no sense to me'. The exhibition must speak to the situation of today as well as to the world of the Bible.
- *It must convey information.* People should be able to go away with a new idea or with an awareness that they had discovered something they did not know before.

There are some organisations which will put on a Bible Exhibition for you but it is probably better to think about planning and organising one yourself. The trouble with having a ready-made exhibition is that all the work is done for you. This may seem very attractive but doing it yourself means that a good many people can be involved and learn a great deal in the process. Organisations such as the Bible Society can be of help and will give you a great deal of practical advice. With a little imagination and skill the parish can produce a very relevant exhibition AND feel that it is theirs.

A Bible Exhibition must have a certain amount of 'back-up'. Someone will need to be around to make sure that any questions are answered, and the whole congregation has to be well informed of what it is all about. It is also a good idea to ensure that there are materials for sale or free handouts available. If a bookstall is not possible a local bookshop could be advised of the exhibition and warned that they might expect some extra customers! Some bookshops, especially those specifically stocking Christian literature, may be willing to come along for a short period with a selection of books for sale.

The example on page 127 is from a parish which decided to mount a do-it-yourself exhibition. They obtained material from the Bible Society, the Catholic Truth Society and a local bookshop. The exhibition was not large but by skilful use of colouring, lighting and layout it had a very powerful effect.

EXAMPLE

THE WORD OF GOD

This Exhibition was arranged at the back of a church in a very prominent position and lasted for two Sundays.

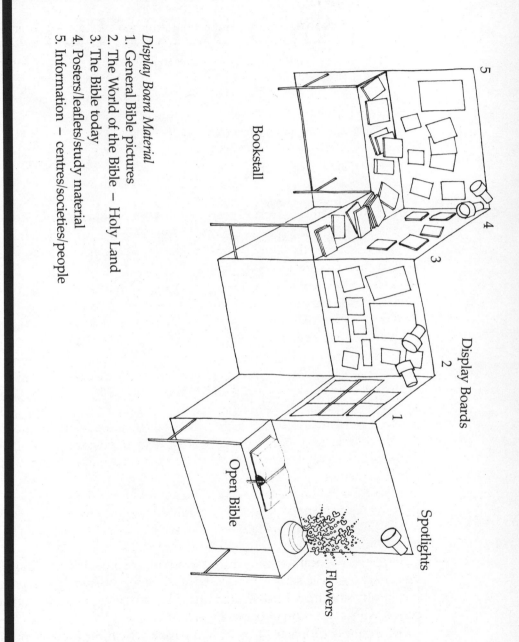

Display Board Material
1. General Bible pictures
2. The World of the Bible — Holy Land
3. The Bible today
4. Posters/leaflets/study material
5. Information — centres/societies/people

Chapter 7

THE INDIVIDUAL AND SCRIPTURE

S O FAR we have concentrated on the use of the Bible in groups of one sort or another. In this chapter we shall look at the place of Scripture for our own individual faith development. This use of the Bible by individuals in the privacy of their own homes is probably the most common way in which the Scriptures are used. Countless generations have been sustained through this means. Reading and meditating on the acts of God as recorded in the Scriptures has enabled them to see his activity in their own lives.

Potential difficulties

There are, however, a number of difficulties for the person, who, as an individual, wishes to use the Bible well.

● *The difficulty of knowing how to interpret the text.* 'How do I know I am not completely wrong?' is a question I am often asked. In a group the problem is lessened because there is a sharing of ideas and interpretation. Extreme views are more easily avoided because members of the group help one another. For the individual there is always the danger of interpreting the text wrongly and 'going off the rails'.

● *The difficulty of knowing which text to explore and which to leave out.* Quite obviously some passages are much more difficult than others. There are some parts of the Bible which are not really suitable for the sort of reading we are considering here. For instance, large chunks of Leviticus are extremely technical and are not likely to give us a great deal of stimulating reading for our prayer. There are two dangers here. The first is taking a book of the Bible and slogging through it, including all the passages which may require quite technical explanation. The reader may well give up trying and end up thinking that the Bible is just too difficult. I have met many people who, with great enthusiasm, started to read at Genesis, intending to work through to the book of Revelation. They usually gave up by the time they reached the end of Deuteronomy – if not before. Some have never opened a Bible since, because they do not know where to look. They need guidance about what to read. The second danger is of going to the opposite extreme, that of only picking the passages which seem to suit us. If we do this we get an unbalanced view of Scripture and we experience the difficulty of seeing it in 'bits'. We find it difficult to get the general sweep of the story or can end of taking passages out of context.

● *The difficulty of overspiritualising the Scriptures.* Using them as a basis for prayer and meditation does not mean that they should not affect the rest of our activity. It is easy to fall into the trap of thinking that reading the Bible is a nice comfortable thing to do. Certainly it is a source of comfort and consolation but it is also full of challenge. Using the Bible for prayer may be very uncomfortable at times!

These difficulties are not insurmountable. There are many good Bible reading notes which can guide the reader, giving a good, balanced 'diet' of texts and notes. This can help to ensure that there is no 'off-the-rails' interpretation. In addition it is possible to obtain Bible reading books for special seasons of the year, such as Lent or Advent. The Bible Reading Fellowship, for instance, produce an excellent range of notes for all ages with contributors from many denominations, along with books for Advent and Lent. In addition to notes there are other methods which individuals can use. Here are four extended examples, all quite different from each other.

EXAMPLE 1   ## EYES, HEART AND HANDS

This method is based on the Sulpician Method taught by Cardinal de Bérulle and outlined by Hubert Northcott CR in his book *The Venture of Prayer* (SPCK, 1962). It has three main parts:

1 Adoration
2 Communion
3 Co-operation

The process helps us meditate on the life of Christ, each of the three stages being summed up in the three clauses of the Lord's Prayer: 'Hallowed be thy name, thy kingdom come, thy will be done'. Here is how Northcott presents it:

1. Adoration – or 'Jesus before the eyes'
As an illustration let us choose the Crucifixion. We think of our Blessed Lord on the cross, picture him hanging there for our salvation. In particular on this occasion we will consider his self-sacrificing love. Then we remind ourselves that this is God incarnate suffering for us; it is the love of God himself revealed here on the cross. Other considerations will occur to us as we bring our minds and imaginations to dwell upon it all. Revelations of the divine love it may be in previous ages, thoughts of the world's sin and our own sin that caused the sacrifice.

As we do this, more and more the wonder and richness of that love will come home to us – the glory of God who thus humbled himself and thus gave himself – the utter worthlessness of ourselves in treating him so. So, the first part of our prayer pours itself out in adoration and thanksgiving before that stupendous revelation. It is an expansion and adaptation of the first clause of the Lord's Prayer, 'Hallowed be Thy Name'.

2. Communion – or 'Jesus in the heart'
We go on to meditate on the desirableness of that love in ourselves. We are conscious of our own selfishness: we realise the necessity of being like our Lord, and how far away we are. Here our thoughts turn to ourselves, but only in the light of God's revelation of love. There can be no room for self-centredness, morbidity or day dreaming in such a context. So our prayer changes into penitence and petition, asking our Lord to come and reign in our hearts. Such communing with him is rightly named communion. But the name has a deeper significance. It is so called because it means that Christ does come and fill our hearts. His grace meets our prayer, and his love takes possession of us.

Now just as the first clause of the Lord's Prayer summed up the first stage of this method, so the second clause sums up this second stage. 'Thy Kingdom come' – the reign of Christ as undisputed king of the soul.

3. Cooperation – or 'Jesus in the hand'
Here we consider how we can cooperate with our Lord to carry into effect his will. It brings us to the third clause of the Lord's Prayer, 'Thy will be done on earth as it is in heaven'. In the mystery of Calvary we have adored God incarnate

on the cross; we have considered the meaning of his love and prayed that it might rule in our hearts. Now we stop to think how we can realise this in action. And care must be taken that our resolutions at the end of our prayer (whatever method we use) should be practical and definite.

EXAMPLE 2 ## USING IMAGINATION

This method makes use of that underestimated gift, the imagination. Quite rightly, we do well to be wary of overdoing this. We can easily get carried away by all sorts of flights of fancy if we are not careful. The results could be disastrous and we could end up deluding ourselves. However, provided we are aware of the danger, the use of the imagination can help us greatly in our times of prayer and meditation. Like the previous method, this way of using Scripture concentrates on the life of Christ (though there is no reason why it should not be used with other suitable parts of the Old or New Testaments).

Step 1
- Spend a while relaxing.
- Concentrate on your breathing; on the sounds you can hear.
- Consciously bring any worries or problems you have before God; tell him of them.
- Ask for his guidance as you read.

Step 2
- Slowly read the chosen passage (make sure it is not too long).
  By way of an illustration let us use Luke 22:39-45.

And he came out, and went, as was his custom, to the Mount of Olives; and the disciples followed him. And when he came into the place he said to them, 'Pray that you may not enter into temptation.' And he withdrew from them about a stone's throw, and knelt down and prayed, 'Father if thou art willing, remove this cup from me; nevertheless not my will, but thine, be done.' And when he rose from prayer he came to the disciples and found them sleeping for sorrow.

Step 3
- Read the text again, trying to picture the scene.
- Now put down your Bible and imagine you are there as one of the disciples.
- Imagine the garden – what is it like, where is Jesus?
- Imagine the disciplines – what do they feel, what do you feel as one of them?
- Imagine Jesus – how do you see him, what is he doing?
- Stay with the picture as long as feels comfortable.

Step 4 Now form a short prayer – or remain in silence with God if you feel no need for words.

Step 5 Pray for others, especially any you know who are distressed or in despair.

Step 6 What do you think God is asking you to do for him in the light of your prayer?

EXAMPLE 3   USING EMPHASIS

The final example is a very simple but effective way of meditating on Scripture. It is important with this method to take a very short verse that can easily be remembered. The method suggests taking the verse, repeating it several times and putting the emphasis on a different word or short phrase of the sentence each time. As with all the methods for individual use it is very important to take time. Do not rush or hurry the process. Allow some time to calm down before you even start.

'I chose you and appointed you that you should go and bear fruit.' (John 15:16)

1. Think for a while about the sentence.

2. Now say it several times so that you can remember it without difficulty.

3. When you are happy with this repeat the sentence several times, putting the emphasis on the word 'I':
'*I* chose you and appointed you that you should go and bear fruit.'

4. When you have done this a few times repeat the sentence, putting the emphasis on the word 'chose':
'I *chose* you and appointed you that you should go and bear fruit.'

5. Continue this process, taking your time and emphasising the words: 'you', 'appointed you', 'should go', 'bear fruit'.

6. Close with a prayer summing up your meditation.

EXAMPLE 4   USING SET TEXTS

Another way of using the Bible alone is to concentrate on the passages set for each Sunday. Those who come from a tradition where the readings for a Sunday are set are offered a ready-made structure. The great advantage of this is that it gives a good balanced approach. The disadvantage is that the individual has to make sense of the text without the aid of set notes or guides. However, it is possible to do this: indeed, some people prefer it. This example takes the reading and asks some basic questions. Using these questions can help to focus our thoughts and prevent us from skirting around the edges of the text.

1 What immediately strikes me?
2 What is the main theme for me?
3 Who are the main characters for me?
4 With whom (or what) do I identify?
5 What question am I being asked through the passage?
6 What difference should it make to my life?

Here is how it works with a particular passage:

1 Kings 19:9-13a

Elijah came to a cave, and lodged there; and behold, the word of the Lord came to him, and he said to him, 'What are you doing here, Elijah?' He said, 'I have been very jealous for the Lord, the God of hosts; for the people of Israel have forsaken thy covenant, thrown down thy altars, and slain thy prophets with the sword; and I, even I only, am left; and they seek my life to take it away.' And he said 'Go forth and stand upon the mount before the Lord.' And behold the Lord passed by, and a great and strong wind rent the mountains, and broke in pieces the rocks before the Lord, but the Lord was not in the wind; and after the wind an earthquake; and after the earthquake a fire, but the Lord was not in the fire; and after the fire a still small voice. And when Elijah heard it, he wrapped his face in his mantle and went out and stood at the entrance to the cave.

1. What immediately strikes me?

(Elijah's aloneness: 'and I, even I only, am left.')
(That God notices Elijah's plight and asks what is wrong.)

2. What is the main theme for me?

(God speaks in an unspectacular way.)

3. Who are the main characters for me?

(God and Elijah — the story stresses that Elijah needs God and that God wants to communicate with Elijah.)

4. With whom or what do I identify?

(With Elijah. I often feel as he did, both in his aloneness, and in his feelings of unworthiness when God communicates himself.)

5. What question am I being asked through this passage?

(Do I hear God in the still small voice?)

6. What difference should it make to my life?

(I should be more conscious, when I feel alone and all is going wrong, that God wishes to communicate himself.)

Helpful hints

When using the Bible for prayer and meditation alone:

● Take your time, no matter what method you use.

● Use a variety of methods. You may prefer some more than others. If you feel you are getting 'stale' try a different approach.

● Make sure your use of the Bible is well balanced. If you can, try to follow some sort of scheme, either of notes or of references.

● Make sure your meditation is related to the rest of your life. End with some thought or prayer that you can take away with you into your everyday situations.

Chapter 8
MORE RESOURCES FOR SCRIPTURE

THIS CHAPTER contains a miscellany of examples of different ways of using Scripture. Each example is complete in itself and, hopefully, the ideas which each embodies provide a basis for groups to develop their own material. There is a brief introduction to each method and a few notes at the end which point out some of the major ways in which each example works. Remember that it is vitally important to adapt any material you may use to meet your own situation. Always be ready to adapt and adapt again according to your own particular needs.

■ EXPLORING IMAGES

This method takes some of the images used in the Bible and explores what they say about our relationship with God and with each other. In this example the images explored focus on the theme of the People of God. Other themes that could be explored might include images of God (e.g. Rock, Warrior, Shepherd, etc.) or images of forgiveness (e.g. lost sheep, wandering son, etc.).

This method is suitable for almost any group. Large groups can be split into smaller units and the method can be used with adults or adapted for use with young people.

EXAMPLE

IMAGES OF CHURCH

Step 1   Spend a moment in quiet reflection.

Step 2   Share with one other person your response to these questions:
- Which groups, other than the Church, do you belong to?
- How, very briefly, would you describe them?
- What impresses you about them?

Step 3   Here is a list of Biblical words or images associated with the group we call the People of God:

Bride of Christ	Purchased people
New Israel	The family of God
God's flock	Branches of the vine
Body of Christ	A holy nation
Temple of the Lord	A wandering tribe
Chosen race	The Temple of God
Field of God	A royal priesthood
Community of the faithful	House of God
A pilgrim people	

Circle three or four in the list which you feel best express what the Church is; show your order of preference and add any other images you wish.

Step 4
- What does your list say about how you visualise the People of God e.g. is it static or on the move?
- What do your images say about God's relationship with his people? Share your responses

Notes

1. Note the use of sharing with one other person at the start of the exercise; it avoids a long discussion at what is an introductory stage.
2. Note the use of a list of images or words. This is a very useful way of getting people thinking and can also show the wide variety of images used in Scripture.
3. Note how getting people to pick the images which resonate with them helps them to discover how they themselves visualise the theme.
4. If time permits the group should be encouraged to look up the references to two or three of the images on which most of the members have centred.

■ EXPLORING EXPERIENCES

This method aims to enable people to uncover some of their own experiences of life and to relate this to what God has to say about them in the Scriptures.

It is best used in small groups but is equally useful for groups which have a particular pastoral interest, for instance, a group working with the bereaved, the unemployed or those under stress. This particular example looks at the common experience of coping with failure in our lives, but the method could be used equally well with many other human situations. To explore our own reactions to such situations in the light of Scripture not only may be a source of considerable comfort, but can help us to be more sensitive to the needs of others.

EXAMPLE

SHARING EXPERIENCES OF FAILURE

Step 1   Opening Prayer

Step 2   Carefully read the following; it may be helpful if different people read out each one.

'Now that my marriage has fallen to pieces I just feel totally worthless.'

'I have not had a job for three years. I feel useless, as if it is all my fault and that I am failing my family.'

'Since I retired I feel I am no use to society. I feel I'm just being a burden to my children.'

'I just can't tell anyone else what I have done. I just can't.'

'I look at my teenage children and ask myself, "Where did we go wrong?"'

'I've always felt second best. I was never as clever as my brother.'

'I went there to give her a helping hand and I came away feeling that I had only made things worse.'

Step 3   (This part of the exercise is for your eyes only. You will not have to show it to anyone else.)

Write below any areas of failure you have felt in your own life.

Step 4 Share together how you think the feeling of failure affects a person and those around him or her.

Step 5 The Gospels also express Jesus' experience of coping with the failures of others and with his own doubts. Read each one aloud, slowly and carefully:

> 'My God, my God, why have you forsaken me?'
>
> 'Philip, have I been so long with you and still you do not know me?'
>
> 'When his family heard of this they came to take charge of him saying, "He is out of his mind."'
>
> 'And you, will you also go away?'
>
> 'He was taken out to the place of criminals and there nailed to a cross.'
>
> 'Were not ten cured, where are the other nine?'
>
> 'And many heard this and said, "It is too hard a saying" and walked no more with him.'
>
> 'Crucify him, crucify him!'

Step 6 Discuss together. Which of these statements stands out for you?
1 In what way can we say that Jesus understands our experience of failure?
  Can we say that there are any areas that he would *not* understand?
2 Where is God when you feel a failure?
  Can failure be a positive experience — can it lead to something good; if so, how?

Step 7 Closing prayer or reading.

Notes
1. Note that this method starts with our experience and moves on to the Bible.
2. Note that there is some work done alone and not shared. This can help people isolate certain painful areas without fear that they will have to share it with others.
3. Note the use of reading aloud in different voices. This can add emphasis.
4. Note that the final questions seek to link our experience with that of Christ as portrayed in the Gospels.

■ EXPLORING GIFTS

This is an example of a method which encourages people to discover their own potential. In this case it is the gifts they have amongst them, but it could focus on competencies or strengths and weaknesses. This method usually requires a small group who know each other reasonably well.

EXAMPLE

Spend a moment in prayer.
Think for a moment.
Remember one another in the group before God.

1 In groups of about eight sit in a circle, each person with a sheet of paper.

2 Write your name at the top, and underneath two or three things you feel you are good at, or the particular gifts which you have.

3 Pass on your sheet to the person on the right and take the sheet from the person on your left.

4 Look at the name and add to the list another gift that you think that person has.

5 Continue the process until your own sheet comes back to you.

6 Read and reflect for a moment on what others have said of you.

7 Share the gifts you have amongst you.

8 One person now reads aloud 1 Cor 12:12-21.

9 Discuss in what ways:
the passage is related to what we have discovered about our gifts;
in what *practical* ways we can ensure that all the gifts that make up parts of the body are used.

Close with a prayer, in silence or spoken aloud, thanking God for one another and for the gifts discovered during this session.

Notes

1. Note the use of working alone in this method and then coming together to share. This is a very valuable way of getting people to explore areas in which they may otherwise be reticent about sharing, and getting everyone to participate.

2. Note that the element of discovery is very explicit. People do not know what others might write and can be pleasantly surprised.

3. Note that you could do this type of exploration by asking people to draw rather than write.

4. Note that the last question aims at a *practical* outcome from the exercise. It is always good to include something very positive which enforces the need to relate our discoveries to our situation.

EXAMPLE ■ **EXPLORING OUR WORTH**

This method looks at our own personal development and sees it reflected in Scripture.

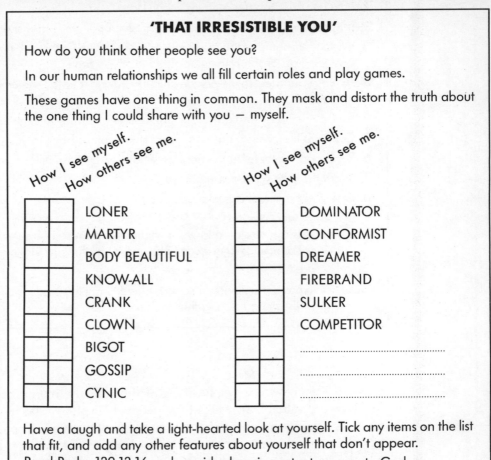

'THAT IRRESISTIBLE YOU'

How do you think other people see you?

In our human relationships we all fill certain roles and play games.

These games have one thing in common. They mask and distort the truth about the one thing I could share with you — myself.

How I see myself.
How others see me.

LONER
MARTYR
BODY BEAUTIFUL
KNOW-ALL
CRANK
CLOWN
BIGOT
GOSSIP
CYNIC

How I see myself.
How others see me.

DOMINATOR
CONFORMIST
DREAMER
FIREBRAND
SULKER
COMPETITOR
....
....
....

Have a laugh and take a light-hearted look at yourself. Tick any items on the list that fit, and add any other features about yourself that don't appear.
Read Psalm 139:13-16 and consider how important you are to God.

Notes
1. Note the use of humour in the method.
2. Note the flexibility of the method: it can be used either individually or in small or large groups, for adults or young people.
3. The method is open-ended enough to allow people to share their list of characteristics or not, as seems right.

■ **EXPLORING MISSION**

This method explores the theme of witness through our own experiences of witness and consideration of the ways in which Jesus shared his message. The example which follows is taken from *Telling my story, sharing my faith* by Anne Bishop and Eldon Hay (Division of Mission in Canada, United Church of Canada).

I. COMMUNITY

TELLING MY STORY: THE PEOPLE I TOUCH   (5-10 minutes)

Step 1   List all the persons you were in touch with this past week. Don't forget store clerks, telephone operators, garage attendants as well as friends and family! Add up the number of people on your list.

Step 2   As a total group, add up the number of people you came into contact with over the past week. Are you surprised at the number?

II. LEARNING TIME

A. HOW DID JESUS SHARE HIS MESSAGE?   (30 minutes)

Jesus shared his message in a variety of ways and in a variety of situations.

Step 1   List on large sheets of paper as many different ways as you can think of in which Jesus shared his message.

Step 2   Give each person one or more of the following passages of Scripture. Have them read the passage(s) and write down the method that Jesus used to share his message:

Matt 5:1,2	Matt 21:12,13
Mark 14:32-34	John 1:37-39
Luke 4:33-37	Matt 23:13-15
Mark 4:33	John 2:1,2
Matt 19:13-15	Matt 9:10,11
John 3:1-6	Matt 4:24

Step 3   If any of these are not on your newsprint list, add them.

B. HOW DO I COMMUNICATE MY FAITH?   (10-15 minutes)

Step 1   Individually, list the different ways in which you communicate your faith.

Step 2   Look again at the list of people you were in touch with this week.
How did you show your faith to them?
How could you show more of your faith to them?

Step 3   Would any of them especially appreciate or benefit from an expression of your faith in word or action? Who?
What would be an appropriate way to express your faith to them?

Step 4   Share whatever you wish of Steps 1 and 2 with one other person.

III. REFLECTION   (5-10 minutes)

Were there surprises for you in this session? What were they?

Are you an evangelist in more ways than you thought? What are they?

Do you have more situations for evangelism than you thought? What are they?

How can you be a more effective, more sensitive evangelist?

Notes

1. Note the use of brainstorming – listing on large sheets of paper. This is useful early on in a session because people can respond off the tops of their heads, and often it brings to light both the obvious, which may remain unsaid, and the deeply hidden which people may be afraid to share in a discussion.

2. Note the use of a whole range of Scripture passages. This method builds up a picture of the 'theme'.

3. Note the practical application at the end of the session.

■ EXPLORING WORDS

Taking one word and tracing it through Scripture can add a wealth of meaning to a common theme. This example uses the word 'bread' but the possibilities are endless. The method can be used by small groups and, if combined with the use of pictures or music, the impact can be even greater. Such a method can be used with all ages, and the word in people's own experiences can be integrated with the word as used in Scripture, so that new potential for meaning and experience can be revealed.

EXAMPLE   BREAD FOR THE WORLD

Step 1   Have a loaf of bread as a focal point, with perhaps a lighted candle or a small flower arrangement beside it.

Step 2   Let various people read out the passages, leaving time between each one.

1. I am the bread of life. This is the bread that comes down from heaven so that a man may eat it and not die. (John 6:48-50)

2. What father among you would hand his son a stone when he asked for bread? (Matt 7:9)

3. Philip, where can we buy bread, to feed all these people? (John 6:5)

4. Man does not live on bread alone but on every word that comes from the mouth of God. (Matt 4:4)

5. Unless a grain of wheat falls on the ground and dies, it remains only a single grain. But if it dies, it yields a rich harvest. (John 12:24)

6. No matter how many of us there are, we all eat from the same loaf, showing that we are parts of the one body of Christ. (1 Cor 10:17)

7. I am the bread of life. He who comes to me will never be hungry, he who believes in me will never thirst. (John 6:35)

8. They knew him in the breaking of bread. (Luke 24:35)

9. My tears have become my bread. (Psalm 42:3)

10. As the rain and snow come down from heaven and stay upon the ground to water the earth and cause the grain to grow and produce seed for the farmer and bread for the hungry, so also is my word, I send it out and it always produces fruit. (Is 55:10-11)

11. Don't worry about things – food, drink, clothes . . . Look at the birds: they don't worry about what they are going to eat . . . For your heavenly Father feeds them, and you are far more valuable . . . (Matt 6:25-26)

12. He took the bread and broke it and gave it to them.

Step 3   Allow time for reflection.

Step 4   Discuss what the readings tell us about:
(a) the image of bread
(b) why it is important for us
(c) God's dealings with us
(d) our dealings with each other.

Step 5   Share stories of particular meals which stand out as important in your own experience. If the group is small each member could tell of the meal they remember best. Why is sharing meals together important for us?

Notes
1. Note the use of a focal point to help set the atmosphere and concentrate attention.
2. Note the link between our experience and the Scriptures.
3. Note the use of many readings.
4. Note the use of both Old and New Testaments.

■ EXPLORING WITH QUESTIONS

This method is based on the Gospel Enquiry sessions developed by Family and Social Action. There is a basic scheme and it can be applied to most Gospel incidents. In preparing the Gospel Enquiry either as a leader or a group member you may find the following points helpful:

● What is happening?
● What does this tell us about Jesus?
● Do the same things happen to me?

EXAMPLE

1. What is happening?
● When and where did this incident take place? (If necessary do a bit of background reading from the Gospel.)
● What is the attitude of people involved in the passage?
● Who are they? What sort of work do they do? What type of people are they?
● What were the circumstances – were there a lot of people or just a few?

2. What does this tell us about Jesus?

- What is his attitude to the people? How does he act? How does he talk? How does he express his feelings?
- What virtues does he show? How can I learn from his: charity, goodness, sensitivity, understanding, gentleness, strength?

3. Do the same things happen to me?

- Do I meet the same sort of people as those in this passage?
- Can I think of any similar examples? What opportunities have there been in my life for dealing with situations in the way Jesus did?

Notes

1. Note the three clear stages for this method.

2. Note the movement from looking at the text, to Jesus, to me.

3. Note the fact that this method sticks closely to the text and yet allows many different aspects of the passage to become clear.

4. Note that it can easily be used with most Gospel passages (or adapted to many Old Testament incidents).

■ EXPLORING WITH SILENCE

This method makes use of silence and reflection in a group situation, and is suitable for small groups. This particular example takes as its theme 'The Word of God', but other images could easily be used in a similar way.

EXAMPLE   THE WORD OF GOD

Step 1   Put a Bible in a place of honour in the group; perhaps place a lighted candle beside it.

Step 2   After introduction, allow people to settle.

Step 3   Opening prayer.

Step 4   Give everyone a small sheet of stiff card and a pen, and ask them to write (or draw) their favourite verse from Scripture.
Share in twos and threes why this verse was chosen. Why was it powerful?

Step 5   Read, with long silences in between, the following passages:

Your Word, O Lord, is a lamp to my feet and a light to my path. (Ps 119:105)

For this commandment which I command you this day is not too hard for you, neither is it far off. It is not in heaven, that you should say, 'Who will go up for us to heaven, and bring it to us, that we may hear it and do it?' Neither is it beyond the sea, that you should say, 'Who will go over the sea for us, and bring it to us, that we may hear it and do it? But the word is very near you; it is in your mouth and in your heart, so that you can do it. (Deut 30:11-14)

For the word of God is living and active, sharper than any two-edged sword, piercing to the division of soul and spirit, of joints and marrow, and discerning the thoughts and intentions of the heart. And before him no creature is hidden, but all are open and laid bare to the eyes of him with whom we have to do. (Heb 4:12-13)

For as the rain and the snow come down from heaven, and return not thither but water the earth, making it bring forth and sprout, giving seed to the sower and bread to the eater, so shall my word be that goes forth from my mouth; it shall not return to me empty, but it shall accomplish that which I purpose, and prosper in the thing for which I sent it. (Is 55:10-11)

The grass withers, the flower fades; but the word of our God will stand for ever. (Is 40:8)

Is not my word like fire, says the Lord, and like a hammer which breaks the rock in pieces? (Jer 23:9)

'But you, son of man, hear what I say to you; be not rebellious like that rebellious house; open your mouth, and eat what I give you.' And when I looked, behold, a hand was stretched out to me, and lo, a written scroll was in it; and he spread it before me; and it had writing on the front and on the back, and there were written on it words of lamentation and mourning and woe. And he said to me, 'Son of man, eat what is offered to you; eat this scroll, and go, speak to the house of Israel.' So I opened my mouth, and he gave me the scroll to eat. And he said to me, 'Son of man, eat this scroll that I give you and fill your stomach with it.' Then I ate it; and it was in my mouth as sweet as honey. (Ezek 2:8-10, 3:1-3)

In the beginning was the Word, and the Word was with God, and the Word was God. He was in the beginning with God; all things were made through him, and without him was not anything made that was made. In him was life, and the life was the light of men. The light shines in the darkness, and the darkness has not overcome it.
And the Word became flesh and dwelt among us, full of grace and truth; we have beheld his glory, glory as of the only Son from the Father. (John 1:1-5, 14)

Step 6 Discuss:
What stands out for you from these passages and why?
What do they say about the purpose and power of Scripture?

Leader: 'Let us remember that God speaks to us through his Word. It is he who is present.'

Step 7 Silent reflection.

Step 8 Each person should place their own Scripture verse around the Bible and reverence it in whatever way they choose.

Suggested family activity

Some families have their Bible open in a place of honour in their home. Each night a different member of the family might bring to the meal table a passage he or she really likes, and read it aloud before dinner.

Notes
1. Note the atmosphere of prayer.
2. Note the fact that in this method the Bible is allowed to speak for itself.
3. Note the use of actions as well as words in this example.
4. Note the suggested family activity for use after the group. This can help create a link between the group work and our family life.

■ EXPLORING OUR COMMUNITY

This method helps us to look at our Church community, at strong and weak points and at how we should work together. The example which follows is taken from *Telling my story, sharing my faith* by Anne Bishop and Eldon Hay (Division of Mission in Canada, United Church of Canada).

EXAMPLE

I. COMMUNITY

TELLING MY STORY: LIVING IN MY BODY   (5-10 minutes)

When Paul describes the community of Christian believers, he calls it the Body of Christ. In this session we will explore Paul's concept of the Body, but first we will spend some time looking at the image itself.

Step 1   Working alone, write down the parts of your body which have limited you most (bad back, injuries, weak heart etc.).

....

....

Now write down what you have learned from your weaker or limited parts (i.e. while in hospital I learned patience etc.).

....

....

Step 2   Write down the parts of your body which have been most important to you in reaching your goals (hands for a carpenter, eyes for someone who likes reading etc.).

....

....

Now in what ways have your strong parts been a disadvantage (i.e. I was a good athlete, but that kept me from being a good student etc.)?

....

....

Step 3   Share with one other person.

II. LEARNING TIME

A. THE BODY OF CHRIST   (10-15 minutes)

Paul speaks of Christians being parts of the Body of Christ. In the Body, we are all different and serve different functions, but each of us is vital to the whole. The animating force of the Body, its soul, is the Holy Spirit. In I Cor 12 Paul describes the Body and the gifts which the Spirit gives to members of the Body. In I Cor 13 he talks about the most important gift of the Spirit.

Step 1   Read aloud I Cor 12:12-27 and I Cor 13.

Step 2   In pairs, take a few moments to share your feelings about these passages.

B. IMPLICATIONS OF BEING IN THE BODY   (10-15 minutes)

'Now you are the body of Christ and individually members of it.' (I Cor 12:27)

We are members of the Body of Christ. We are going to look at a passage of Scripture and ask what we are challenged to be or to become when we belong to the Body of Christ.

Step 1   Look at the following Scripture passage: Galatians 5:22 – 6:2
Complete the following sentence on a large piece of paper.

'This passage says that, as part of the Body of Christ, we are called to:

....

Step 2   Discuss:
Paul stresses the gentle nature of a Christian, and yet Jesus was not always gentle. He hurled insults at the scribes and Pharisees, troubled the sensitivities of good people by associating with prostitutes and sinners, defied religious law, and turned over the tables of the money changers in the temple. Is a Christian ever called to be angry, impatient, rebellious? Under what circumstances?

C. GIFTS (25–30 minutes)

The Holy Spirit gives each of us special gifts to contribute to the Christian community. It is important that we come to see our own gifts and those of others. 'Now there are varieties of gifts but the same Spirit' (1 Cor 12:4).

Step 1   Someone reads again I Cor 12:12-27.

Step 2   On your own, write down what you think is your particular talent or gift.

Step 3   Share together.

III. REFLECTION

In a moment of silence, look back over the session.
What discoveries have you made about yourself?
What discoveries have you made about the Church?

Notes
1. Note that the method can be used with people as individuals, in pairs or as a group.
2. Note the use of writing things down. This can help to clarify ideas succinctly.
3. Note the way the session begins with a consideration of the *image* Paul uses and links it to our own experience.
4. Note how the passage is read more than once.

■ EXPLORING WITH PROVERBS

The English language is full of sayings and proverbs. Many have Biblical parallels. This method could be used with other well-known sayings apart from proverbs, even with TV advertisement slogans! It is important not to overstress the use of the imagination or to distort the Biblical parallels to make them fit the text. Provided that this is remembered this method can prove a very useful starting point for deeper exploration.

EXAMPLE

'FROM TINY ACORNS MIGHTY OAK TREES GROW'

1 Discuss:
What do you think this proverb means? How do we develop? Jot down three experiences which have helped you to grow in the past: one from your childhood, one as a young person, and one from your adult life. Share your findings together.

2 Now look at a Biblical parallel.

He said, therefore, 'What is the kingdom of God like? And to what shall I compare it? It is like a grain of mustard seed which a man took and sowed in his garden; and it grew and became a tree, and the birds of the air made nests in its branches.' (Luke 13:18-19)

What does this passage say about growing in faith?
Are there any other Biblical parallels?

Notes

1. Note the simplicity of this method.

2. Note the scope for discovering more than one appropriate Biblical text. This can help to ensure that the parallel is not stretched too far.

3. Note that many other proverbs could be used. These might include:

'All that glitters is not gold.'

'Never put off till tomorrow what you can do today.'

'It's a case of the blind leading the blind.'

'Beauty is in the eye of the beholder.'

'Look before you leap.'

'Many hands make light work.'

'You cannot have your cake and eat it.'

■ EXPLORING OUR REACTIONS

This method looks at a present-day situation in the form of a 'case study' and then reflects upon it in the light of Scripture. It is one of a series from Grail Publications, *Six Discussion Meetings for Small Groups* (1970).

EXAMPLE

HERE AND NOW

"Mr Andrew Dobbs, aged 79, lives with his niece Mary and her husband, an arrangement of some fifteen year's standing. It has worked out satisfactorily because he is a keen gardener and has taken over the large garden as his responsibility, thereby reducing the fruit and vegetable bills and keeping himself well occupied. Now, however, the situation is changing: Mary's four children are growing up and need more room. Mr Dobbs' arthritis is beginning to prevent his activity in the garden and has made him not only less able to look after himself, but much more difficult temperamentally. He is becoming a constant source of irritation and disagreement within the household.

Mary and her husband feel they owe it to the children to get Uncle Andrew into an old people's home and so preserve the harmony of their own. Uncle Andrew is made very unhappy by the idea and goes into the home much against his will, despite assurances that he will be well looked after by a competent staff and that the family will visit him frequently. Mary and her husband feel very guilty when they know he is so miserable."

Could they have acted otherwise?

Talking points

1 Has love to be worked out or is it something which simply exists or does not exist between people? Does it grow?

2 What factors hinder us from expressing love for people? Why are most of us afraid to love?

3 Is the love of one's neighbour, spoken of by Christ, a different kind of love from the human love we experience?

4 How do we express our love for God? Should we have a different relationship to the Father, the Son and the Holy Spirit?

5 Do our individual actions for good or evil affect the community? When we fail is there anything we can do?

Scripture enquiry

Read: I Cor 13:1-7.

Discuss this passage in relation to our personal lives, the parish, the local community, other Christians.

Notes

1. Note the use of the case study at the beginning. This can often help to 'earth' the topic.

2. Note the fact that the talking points allow time for this to be thoroughly thought through before the Bible passage is introduced.

3. Note that the talking points raise a wide variety of questions. Not all these need be considered as long as sufficient time is allowed in which to discuss the problem.

■ EXPLORING WITH STORY

He was sitting on the floor hugging his knees, a six-year-old bundle of mischief with an insatiable appetite for finding out who, what, where, when and how! Totally absorbed in the story his face registered the emotions of excitement, suspense and fear. 'And then it happened,' said the storyteller. 'His foot slipped and Terry felt himself slipping down and down the cliff towards the rocks and the sea below.' He had heard the story before but the suspense was still there. Would anything save his hero from certain death?'

★

They were sitting in a circle: seven adults, listening to and yet not absorbed in what was being said. No excitement or emotion registered on their faces. 'And the storm came down on the lake,' said the storyteller, 'and they were filling with water. And they went and woke him, saying, "Master, we are perishing." '

★

Two stories, in some ways very similar, and yet the reactions on the part of the hearers were very different. It is not very often that an adult hearing a Bible passage experiences the same sort of involvement as the six-year-old in his story. And yet the Bible is shot through again and again with stories — stories which should not only attract our attention but in which we should become involved.

Importance of stories

Stories are very important to us. They are a natural and vital part of the way in which we learn and make sense of our world. We discover many truths by sharing stories, telling stories and listening to them. By telling the tale of what has happened to us we clarify and reassess our own understanding of the experience and its effect on us. By listening to the stories of others we identify similar experiences in our own lives and continue to make sense of them. Sometimes we shall gain new understanding or a new awareness of how we ourselves tick. This concept of story is so important in our use of Scripture that it is worthwhile to explore the story theme a little more closely before we give an example of how story can be used.

Some concepts are best described or handed on in story form rather than through definitions. Some of our noblest ideas, such as courage, love or unselfishness, can only be truly expressed in depth by means of story. When I want to explain what courage is I tend not to give the dictionary definition but to tell a tale which illustrates courage. Naturally, therefore, we should expect to find many ideas about God in Scripture embodied in story form.

The use of story in our work with Scripture offers endless possibilities with all ages. Using story in Bible activity is important because:

- It helps us reshape and rethink our own experiences of God. It helps us to give order to what we think and feel.

- We can identify some of our own stories in the Bible story. My story and my life are linked in a very real way with the story of God's activity. In a sense the story becomes my story and my story is to be found in God's story. This linking of our stories with God's story is vital. Firstly, it takes me out of myself and reminds me I am part of God's wider activity; secondly, it gives me a sense of identity, reminding me where I have come from, to whom I belong.

- It has not always been realised that people are natural storytellers. This is how we function and how we learn from each other.

Uses of story

Stories can be used in many different ways. For instance:

- People can be encouraged to share their own stories.
- People can be encouraged to share the stories of others.
- People can be encouraged to share favourite stories from literature.
- People can be encouraged to share favourite stories in the form of art or photographs.

● People can be encouraged to tell stories for the simple pleasure of immersing themselves in them just as they would with a favourite piece of music.

Here, then, is one example of how story can be used. It shows how an individual story was seen in the light of God's story and what it might mean for those in the group.

EXAMPLE

THE UGLY DUCKLING

Step 1   Coming together
Welcome and introductions (if necessary).

Step 2   Our Story
The leader or a group member tells the story of the Ugly Duckling.

Discuss: What do you think the story tells us? You will probably get several answers coming through, including:
● it is about our potential to be greater than we are
● it is about beauty coming from unexpected sources
● it is about change and alteration
● it is about self-discovery.

Step 3   My Story
In pairs, share your own stories. Share one experience when you discovered a new outlook on who you are.

Step 4   The Jesus Story
As a group, read the Parable of the Mustard Seed (Luke 13:18-19).
● How does this story of Jesus relate to what we have discussed so far?
● In what ways can we grow towards our full potential? Be practical!

Step 5   Reflections
On your own, jot down *one* practical activity which you think will help you develop as a person.

Notes
1. Note the use of secular, Gospel and personal stories.
2. Note the practical implications at the end of the session. It is always good to ensure that the session helps people progress in relating their daily lives to the work done in the group.
3. Note that the method uses individual, pair and group work.

Chapter 9

PROBLEMS AND PITFALLS WITH SCRIPTURE

Ten Common Problems

■ TEN COMMON PROBLEMS

Using Scripture in the local church is not all plain sailing; sooner or later problems are bound to arise. Naturally these will vary according to the individual situation, but in this chapter we will consider ten of the most common difficulties. They are not in any order of priority; they are simply ten of the problems which I have discovered that most groups and local congregations have to cope with at some time or another. For each problem there will be some practical hints which should help towards overcoming the difficulty.

1. 'We have some very odd interpretations in our group.'
THE PROBLEM OF MISHANDLING THE TEXT

As we have already seen elsewhere, one of the real difficulties of using Scripture is that no Bible reading is neutral. We all interpret the text according to our own life experience, education and culture. Sooner or later many Biblical activities encounter the problem that people are manipulating the text to say what they want it to say. The text is mishandled in order to prove a point. Often it is taken out of context. The setting in which the passage was originally conceived is ignored or the original meaning of the writer is disregarded. Scripture is used to justify a pet theory or to give authority to a particular viewpoint, regardless of the teaching of the Church or the wisdom of countless generations of Christians down through the ages. What, then, can be done to ensure that the text is not mishandled either by an individual in a group or by a section of the local congregation?

Helpful hints

There are at least three ways of helping to overcome this problem.

1. Ensure that the text is put into its context. Look at the situation for which it was written. Look at the findings of Biblical scholars. Ask yourself, 'Why was this text written?', 'To whom was it addressed?' Ask yourself, above all, 'What is the major theme of this passage?' and make sure that you see it in its context.

2. Keep in mind what the rest of Scripture has to say about the particular topic under discussion. Look at the theme in other passages. What do other passages with this theme tell us about God or about our relationships with other people? You may, of course, find contradictions, but it is important to ensure that you do not regard one verse or one short passage about a theme as the Bible's entire word on the matter.

3. It is important to weigh up our interpretation of a text against what the Church has to say about the issue under discussion. We have the wisdom of many centuries behind us. If our interpretation is totally opposed to what the Church has always taught then it is likely that we are misinterpreting the Bible. We are rather like the mother who, watching her son march down the road amongst his platoon of soldiers and noticing that he was out of step with everyone else, said, 'My Johnnie's in step; it's the rest of the platoon that are wrong.'

2. 'Our group seems to be going dead on us.'
THE PROBLEM OF 'STALE' GROUPS

This is a very common problem, especially with small groups which have existed for some time. Often these groups comprise the same people who have met regularly for a considerable length of time and who know each other extremely well. There is a feeling that, even before a member opens his or her mouth, the rest of the group knows what he or she is going to say! Usually such groups have had few or no newcomers since they were formed. They enjoy meeting together but have come to the stage at which to go on meeting seems somewhat irrelevant, because no one seems to be getting anything out of the meetings. They have reached an impasse.

Helpful hints

1. Have you been using the same method or type of Bible work throughout your existence, or have you tried different ways of opening up the Scripture? Using a variety of methods can sometimes help the group to keep a sense of freshness.

2. Have you been specific in what you have been trying to do? Groups often get stale because they can see no purpose in meeting. We all work better if we have a specific aim. Try choosing a particular theme which you can discuss for three or four sessions and which has practical applications.

3. Does the rest of the local church community know about you and what you are trying to do? People find it very difficult to join an established group. The lines of communication have to be kept open so that new members can join without feeling that they are intruding. Try writing an article for your parish magazine or bulletin, explaining who you are and what you do; again, be specific.

4. Is it time you had a rest? It is sometimes necessary to let a group die. We should not feel guilty about this. It may be best to allow the group to cease functioning for a while and then to reformulate it with a clear aim and with a particular plan in mind.

5. Are you asking too much of people? It is very difficult for people to join a group if they feel they will be committed week after week without any end in sight. Groups often go stale because they have not taken into account the need to work on some sort of termly basis. In practice it seems far better to work for, say, six or eight weeks in a row and then have a break, restarting the group for another new term with perhaps a new subject and a new method. In this way new people can join without feeling they are overcommitting themselves, and people can drop out without feeling guilty.

3. 'We don't know which Bible to use.'
THE PROBLEM OF CHOOSING TRANSLATIONS

One of the blessings of our generation is the wealth of Bible translations available to us. However, this abundance of versions does have its drawbacks. It is difficult to know which one to use. There are times when it can be an advantage to have many translations available for use in a group, whilst on other occasions it can be a positive disadvantage. Sometimes we need all to share the same text. Then there is the question of which translation is the most accurate, or which is best for reading out loud, or which is best for devotional use.

Helpful hints

1. What are you choosing a translation for? Are you primarily looking for a translation for use in a study group, in a sharing group, in a readers' group for use in liturgy, in an ecumenical group, or for devotional use? The translation you choose will largely depend on the answer to this question.

2. The following guidelines may help you to choose the most appropriate translation:

The Revised Standard Version is generally regarded as the most accurate translation from the Greek and Hebrew. It is, in my experience, the best translation for use in a Bible Study group in which you wish to stick closely to the text and are using commentaries of one sort or another.

The Jerusalem Bible is the version used in the Roman Catholic liturgy, so it is the best translation for those involved in reading at Mass, for liturgy groups and for readers' meetings.

The Good News Bible 'reads' well and is good for Bible Sharing groups, for use with young people and for devotional activities. Its attractive line drawings are an asset.

The Common Bible was produced in 1973 as an ecumenical publication. It is really the Revised Standard Version together with the Apocryphal books and is very useful for ecumenical groups.

The Living Bible is really only a paraphrase rather than an accurate translation. It also tends to have a particular theological interpretation of the text, so it should be handled with great care.

3. Does the method you are using require one or more translations of the Bible? Often it is good to have many different versions around so that you can compare, but do remember that sometimes, for some methods, you will all require the same translation.

4. 'Someone in our group takes it all so literally.'
THE PITFALL OF FUNDAMENTALISM

This problem can cause real difficulty and heartbreak in many groups. Often there are one or perhaps two persons in a small group who believe that every word of the text must be taken absolutely literally. Others may wish to explore what the text has to say but feel held back because the fundamentalist approach assumes that there are no questions to be asked. The real difficulty here is how to handle the situation. It is not just a question of coping with the interpretation that is being given; it is also a question of dealing with the deeply-held beliefs of people within the group.

Helpful hints

1. Use various methods. Sometimes people can be helped to see the Scriptures in a new light if a different method is used. The best methods when this problem arises are those which take a text and try to see it *as a whole*. It may, for instance, be helpful to use a method which asks the group to look at all the characters in a passage. What are they doing? What attitudes are they displaying? How are they reacting to the situation? Often the fundamentalist approach is a very narrow one. Helping people to see the range of attitudes and reactions in a text can perhaps lead them to recognise the diversity and richness that the Bible has to offer.

2. Try not to get into an argument! Arguing seldom helps the situation. Often the views of one person can become paramount within a group, and out of proportion. Try to ensure that the views and the opinions of every person present are known. This will help keep things in their right perspective.

3. Most important of all, ensure that you ask the right questions of the text. Frequently, a fundamentalist approach can be overcome when people realise that the question being asked of the Scriptures is not *how* but *why*. The Bible was not given to us to answer questions as, '*How* did God create the world?' or, ''*How* did the Israelites enter Canaan?' or, '*How* did Jesus rise from the dead?' Instead the questions we should be asking of the text are, '*Why* did God create the world?' or '*Why* did Jesus rise from the dead?' Asking the right questions invariably opens up a whole new world for people to explore.

5. 'We always seem to be pulling the Bible to pieces.'
THE PITFALL OF LIBERALISM

This is the opposite problem to the previous one. Instead of a literal, fundamentalist approach there is an over-liberal attitude towards the Scriptures. The Bible becomes an interesting textbook, a book of examples which we can choose to accept or neglect at will. God seems to have very little to do with it. Analysing, criticising and dissecting the text are all legitimate and valuable ways of getting deeper into it, but if this is *all* there is to our Bible study then we are missing its main purpose. We shall end up with a very patchy and, possibly, disillusioned view of what Scripture is for.

Helpful hints

1. Look for the main theme within a passage before you start analysing its constituent parts. It may be helpful to use some sort of marking technique, asking people to put a question mark where they have found a part of the text which raises questions for them, a tick for those areas and parts of the passage which resonate with them, and an arrow where the passage seems to be suggesting that they are being called to do something specific. This can help people see the passage as a whole and not end up unable to see the wood for the trees.

2. Always ensure that you look at the passage in its context and at other Biblical passages which seem to have the same theme.

3. Again, use a variety of methods. Move about from Bible Study to Bible Sharing methods, from an intellectual approach to a more devotional one.

6. 'The Bible does not really relate to our lives.'
THE PROBLEM OF OVERSPIRITUALITY

This situation arises where an individual, a group, or a local community look at the Bible in too pietistic a way. The Word of God is seen to be speaking only to one aspect of our lives, namely the spiritual. There is little understanding of its message for social justice, for the spreading of the kingdom, or for giving us the strength we need to live a full Christian life in God's world. This is an extremely common problem and one which should constantly be guarded against. The Bible is not just about me and God, or even us and God: it is the story of God's immersion in his world and the implications which this has for us as individuals and as a community.

Helpful hints

1. Ensure that you use methods which connect the Bible with the world in which we live.

2. Make sure that you use methods in which people's daily experiences and the Bible are seen to be interwoven with each other: for instance, the sharing of stories of our own experiences told alongside Biblical stories of a similar type.

3. Ask yourself why this situation has arisen. What does the fact that you have this dichotomy say about you as individuals, about your relationship with the world, and about you as a community in the mission you have to undertake in society? Some Biblical work which considers the relationship between the chosen people, God and the world may help you to see the importance of being more involved.

7. 'Working with the Bible is all too difficult and academic.'
THE PROBLEM OF INTELLECTUALISING

There are very many people within our local churches who would echo this statement that the Bible is too difficult for them to understand. Many of them may never have been involved in any Biblical work at all. They have simply been given the impression from some source or other that working with Scripture, discovering what it is about and gaining strength from it are all beyond them. Others in our local churches would echo this statement because that has been their actual experience. They have belonged to groups where the emphasis has been on the academic and intellectual. They have experienced the Bible as too difficult. For both groups of people there is a barrier to be overcome. Whole sections of our communities have been cut off from discovering the depth of the Bible. Many have become apathetic, others now have an active dislike, many suffer from a sense of guilt. In short, the Bible is a closed book for them.

Helpful hints

1. Try doing things with the Bible for the whole community. Make it too easy rather than too difficult. Give people a 'taster' which will wet their appetites for more.

2. Use visual or audio techniques to open up the Bible for people.

3. In small groups ensure that the methods used are experiential and closely linked to life experience. Make use of story or drama.

4. Do not go in for Biblical criticism at this stage. Do not start dissecting the passages that you are using. Help people simply to discover its main message for them.

8. 'We're fed up with hearing about the Bible.'
THE PITFALL OF OVER-KILL

There are some individuals and some local communities who go overboard on the use of Scripture. Although I believe it to be profoundly true that God's revelation of himself as recorded in the Bible should be at the centre of our lives, this does not mean that the use of Scripture should be dragged into every single thing that we do! Where Scripture becomes a hobby-horse, or where its use is out of proportion, then it is calculated to put people off. Often it becomes a 'thing' in itself. It has no real link either with the Church's tradition or with the Church's life in the world. The classic example is believing that we must have a Scripture reading before every single meeting, simply because we have been told that the Bible is so important. All too frequently it is neither relevant nor appropriate. People can become Gospel-hardened and have an active dislike of the Bible if it is used wrongly or irrelevantly.

Helpful hints

1. Ask yourself whether using Scripture is relevant in a particular situation. It is important to avoid dragging it in on every occasion.

2. Ensure that particular Scriptural events only take place occasionally. Bible Weeks, Bible Retreats or Bible Exhibitions should be *special* events and not part of the church's regular life.

3. Do not try to force everybody to go to a Bible Study group. It is not everyone's cup of tea. Make sure that you have a range of Scriptural activities: some for individuals, some for small groups and some for the whole community, so that people can join or not according to their temperament. If people are made to think that they should be a member of a small group or that they should be at the weekly Bible Study, they are also likely to be forced into feeling guilty if they do not attend.

4. Make sure that any small group work is done on a termly basis and not week in and week out.

9. 'I never get anything out of reading the Bible.'
THE PROBLEM OF BOREDOM

The primary reason that people feel the Bible is boring is that they find it difficult to see how it can relate to them and their lives. This problem of irrelevance is very real. People find it extremely hard to see how words written so many centuries ago and addressed to a culture very different from our own can have anything important to say in our modern, twentieth-century, technological world. It is, perhaps, particularly true of the Old Testament where the gap seems even greater. There are two important points here. The first is that people are often confused about what to do with the text. They believe it to be important but when they read it they see that it bears little resemblance to their own situation. It does not seem to be speaking to them. They are tempted, therefore, to dismiss it as irrelevant or boring. The second point is that people are not encouraged to ask the right questions of the text, and therefore they become even more confused. The real-life questions they wish to ask seem to have no place. The Bible appears to be scratching where they are not itching!

Helpful hints

1. For individuals, encourage them to use a good set of Bible reading notes which will give some idea of the context of the passage and perhaps ask some questions which relate to their life experience.

2. Encourage individual use which is varied. Help people to see that it is good to experiment with various ways of using the Scriptures in devotion.

3. In small groups, encourage people to share openly why they find Scripture difficult. It may be that they are confused by the picture it gives of God, that they find it difficult to cope with the contradictions within Scripture, or that they have trouble relating to the culture of so long ago.

4. Give people the experience of handling Scripture in all sorts of different ways in a group.

5. Make sure that Scripture and life experience are closely interwoven in any method you can.

6. In the wider community ensure that some teaching is given and some explanation offered about what Scripture is, what it is for and, above all, the practicalities of how to use it. This might be done through the parish magazine or bulletin, through sermons, or through a day conference.

10. 'Our group never seems to attract anyone new.'
THE PROBLEM OF INTROVERSION

The problem of encouraging new people into a small group is by no means confined to those dealing with the Bible. If new members are never coming into a group there is a danger of stagnation and, eventually, death. The acute problem of cliques developing within a local church community must also be foreseen and avoided. All groups within the church need to be open to new members, and all groups must ensure that the rest of the community is fully informed about their activities. When no new members have joined the group a small group using Scripture can become stale and content in its own little world. Of course, some groups with few new members are, none the less, active and open and get a great deal from their meetings. On the whole, these groups are the ones in which people are involved in a range of activities outside the small group, and which are usually at pains to ensure that the whole of the local church is aware of their existence and what they are aiming to do. The real problem lies with the introverted group which does not really wish to have new members, or which cannot succeed in recruiting new members if it does wish to have them.

Helpful hints

1. Consider why your group has failed to attract anyone new. Is it because people do not know that you exist, or what you do? Is it because they have a misconception of what you are about? Is it because you really do not want anybody?

2. Should you stop meeting for a while and then reform? This would give new members a chance to join without feeling that they were intruding.

3. How good is your communication with the local church? Would it be a good idea to explain fully what you are about and encourage people to join by both a general and a personal invitation?

4. Consider whether your group offers a method of Bible study which people are finding truly helpful. Should you try a different approach in order to attract new people?

5. Consider working for two or three weeks on one theme at an easy level, so that people can come in order to taste and see if this is for them before they feel they are committing themselves.

A checklist of dos and don'ts

Here is a final checklist which should enable you to avoid some of the major pitfalls and to have a positive approach to Scripture within the local church.

Don'ts

- Don't think the Bible is a magic book with all the answers to all the problems.

- Don't use the Bible just to prove a point, whether it be to enforce a particular view or to back an argument. Never use the Bible to 'proof text' a particular point of view.

- Don't get bogged down too much with the intricacies of biblical criticism. Discoveries from such questions are vital and can help enormously, but always remember that such a method will be foreign to the vast majority of people, and to master it requires time and education.

- Don't think of, let alone use, the Bible as if it were a textbook. It should not be read for facts but as a story. Some things can only be taught through stories, and working with Scripture should enable God's story and ours to become one. Make sure you ask the right questions of the text.

- Don't remove anything from the text, omit bits which are difficult, or isolate verses out of context. Such action leads to a manipulation of the passage and its meaning.

- Don't add anything to the text. It is easy to add our own comments on what 'must have been'. You can end up with people laying more stress on their comments than on the text!

- Don't overspiritualise the Bible. True Biblical work requires that we ask social questions. Scripture needs to be interpreted, not just for our sake alone, but for the sake of others.

- Don't generalise. The passage or text will have little impact on us if we always consider it as happening or involving 'them' or 'people in general'. Scripture should push us to answer real, personal questions such as, 'When did I last act in that way?'

- Don't use Scripture simply to back up doctrine. It gives the impression that the Bible is like a telephone directory, useful if you need confirmation of the number!

Dos
- Do use a variety of methods.

- Do let the Bible speak for itself. Sometimes all that is necessary is that a passage is read well and with understanding.

- Do make sure that all Scriptural activity is concerned with more than the spiritual dimension alone. Take a holistic approach.

- Do remember that no Bible reading is neutral. What we discover is profoundly influenced by our heritage, background, experiences and culture. A lot depends on what angle the Bible is read from. Take care not to manipulate it.

- Do remember that the Bible is concerned primarily with people, not with things.

- Do be creative in your use of methods. Adapt, and go on adapting, any material you may find.

- Do try to work on a termly basis with Scripture, at least as far as small groups are concerned. A term of, say, six or eight weeks twice a year can be much more effective than a weekly meeting which seems to have no end.

- Do ensure that your Biblical work is seen to relate to people's life experiences.

Acknowledgements

In the first instance I gratefully acknowledge the following authors and/or publishers for permission to reprint (with varying degrees of adaptation) their material.

Chapter 2   Small groups and Scripture

Example on Amos 5:21–24 (pp. 22–3) and Example on Luke 9:37–43 (p. 25) are based on a structure suggested by the Lumko Programme (© Lumko Missiological Institute, South Africa).

Example 2 'I have called you by your name' (pp. 26–7) is a shortened version of material offered by Peter Dodson in *Towards Contemplation* (© Sisters of the Love of God, SLG Press, Convent of the Incarnation, Fairacres, Oxford OX4 1TB).

Example 'The God of Suffering' (pp. 27–8) and Example 'The call of God' (p. 29) are both adapted from the Lumko Programme.

Section 3 'Leading a small group' (pp. 33–7) is adapted from *Small Group Leadership* (© The Church Army, Independents Road, Blackheath, London SE3 9LG).

Chapter 3   The creative use of Scripture

Example 'Recording interviews' (p. 46) was suggested by an idea in *Mediaplan — Talking straight* (© Bible Society, Stonehill Green, Westlea, Swindon SN5 7DG).

Example 'The elder brother' (pp. 50–1) is based on an idea by Edwin Robinson.

Chapter 4   Parish activities and Scripture

Example on text preparation (pp. 56–7) is based on ideas presented by Etienne Charpentier in *How to read the Old Testament* (1982) (© SCM Press).

Example 'Sharing the light' (pp. 71–4) uses elements taken from the second session of the four session course *Handing on the Faith in the Home* by Mickey and Terri Quinn (© Veritas Family Resources, Veritas Publications, 7–8 Lower Abbey Street, Dublin 1).

Example 'Living Christ today' (pp. 82–4) is taken from *Teenagers Talking* by Moira Leigh (© The Grail, administered by A. P. Watt Ltd, 20 John Street, London WC1N 2DR).

Chapter 5   Children, young people and Scripture

Example 'A home liturgy for Holy Week' (pp. 93–5) is adapted from an *Adult Network Handout*, by H. G. Dickinson (© Very Rev H. G. Dickinson, The Deanery, 7 The Close, Salisbury, Wilts SP1 2EP).

Example 'People who need me' (pp. 96–7) is taken from the Bible Reading Fellowship *Ladder Book no 2: Myself* (© Bible Reading Fellowship, Warwick House, 25 Buckingham Palace Road, London SW1P 0PP).

The section on 'Preparation' including the Example 'I will bring all my friends together' (pp. 97–100) is taken from *Liturgies of the Word* compiled by Paddy Rylands, published by The Grail (© The Grail, administered by A. P. Watt Ltd, 20 John Street, London WC1N 2DR).

Chapter 6   Special events and Scripture

Quotation (p. 120) from *Many Ministries* by Monica Comerford and Christine Dodd (1982) (© CTS Publications, 38–40 Eccleston Square, London SW1V 1PD).

Chapter 7   The individual and Scripture

Example 1 'Eyes, heart and hands' (pp. 130–1) is from *The Venture of Prayer* (© 1950 Hubert Northcott CR, reproduced by permission of SPCK, London).

Chapter 8 More resources for Scripture

Example 'Sharing experiences of failure' (pp. 137–8) is adapted from an idea in *Towards deeper faith*, prepared and published as part of the Pastoral Renewal Programme of the Archdiocese of Adelaide by the Catholic Education Service (© Archdiocese of Adelaide, Catholic Diocesan Centre, 39 Wakefield Street, Adelaide, SA 5000, Australia).

Example 'That irresistible you' (p. 140) is adapted from *What I've always wanted to say* by Gordon Jones, published by the Church Pastoral Aid Society (© Church Pastoral Aid Society).

Example on exploring gifts (pp. 138–9), example on exploring mission (pp. 140–1), example on exploring with silence (pp. 144–5), and example on exploring our community (pp. 146–8) are taken from *Telling my story, sharing my faith* by Anne Bishop and Eldon Hay, published by The Division of Mission in Canada (© The Division of Mission in Canada, United Church of Canada, 85 St Clair Avenue East, Toronto, M4T 1M8, Canada).

Example on exploring with questions (pp. 143–4) is based on the 'Gospel Enquiry' sessions developed by Family and Social Action (© Family and Social Action, 120b West Heath Road, London NW3).

Example on exploring with silence (pp. 144–6) is adapted from *Bread Broken for a New World*, developed by the Centre for Continuing Religious Education, Archdiocese of Adelaide.

Example on exploring our reactions (pp. 149–50) is from one of a series offered in *Six Discussion Meetings for Small Groups*, published by The Grail (© The Grail, administered by A. P. Watt Ltd, 20 John Street, London WC1N 2DR).

Every effort has been made to trace copyright holders and we hope no copyright has been infringed. Pardon is sought and apology made if we have overlooked a copyright, and a correction will be made in any reprint of this book.

My particular thanks go to those individuals who have helped this book come into being: to Father John Ryan of St Marie's Cathedral, Sheffield for his valuable contribution in Chapter 1; to Anne Boyd and Robert Kelly at Geoffrey Chapman for their ready help; and to Susan Wilcock who helped with the ardous task of typing the manuscript.

Finally my thanks go to the lay people, the clergy and the Bishop of the Diocese of Hallam who were so supportive, and all those who worked so enthusiastically with the methods found in these pages.

CHRISTINE DODD

Selected Resources

Books (general)

Charpentier, E., *How to Read the Old Testament*, SCM Press, 1982.

Charpentier, E., *How to Read the New Testament*, SCM Press, 1982.

Drane, J., *Old Testament Story: an illustrated documentary*, Lion Publishing, 1983.

Hunter, A. M., *Introducing the New Testament*, SCM Press, 1972.

Lion Photoguide to the Bible, Lion Publishing, 1983.

Cruden, Alexander, *Complete Concordance to the Old and New Testaments*, Lutterworth Press.

Neil, William, *Bible Commentary*, Hodder & Stoughton, 1973.

The Jerome Biblical Commentary, Geoffrey Chapman, 1969.

Cambridge Bible commentaries (a series of commentaries for individual books of the Bible), Cambridge University Press.

McKenzie, John L., *Dictionary of the Bible*, Geoffrey Chapman, 1966.

Perkins, Pheme, *Reading the New Testament*, Geoffrey Chapman/Paulist Press, 1988.

King, Nicholas, *What is a Gospel?*, Kevin Mayhew, 1982.

Leaflets (general)

All of the following are produced by the Catholic Truth Society, 38–40 Eccleston Square, London SW1V 1PD.

Dei Verbum, CTS Dc361. A translation of Vatican II's Dogmatic Constitution on Divine Revelation. A key document.

Biblical Studies, CTS Sc30. A translation of *Divino Afflante Spiritu*, Pope Pius XII's encyclical which encouraged modern Catholic Scripture study.

Tell Me the Gospel Truth, CTS Sc40. Confronts the question: in what sense is Scripture true?

What is Biblical Spirituality?, CTS Sc41. On putting God's word at the centre of our life.

The Bible in the Life of the Catholic Church, CTS Sc46.

Can We Trust the Gospels?, CTS Sc47.

For small group work

Small Group Leadership, The Church Army.

Dobson, Peter, *Towards Contemplation*, Fairacres Publications.

Hestenes, Roberta, *Using the Bible in Groups*, The Bible Society, 1983.

McConville, Betty, *How to Start a Small Group*, Grail Publications.

Rogers, Carl, *On Encounter Groups*, Penguin.

Weber, Hans Ruedi, *Experiments with Bible Study*, WCC, 1981.

Wink, Walter, *Transforming Bible Study*, SCM Press.

Liturgy

The Bible in the Mass, CTS Sc43. (Out of print.)

Reader's Handbook, CTS D546.

Warne, Clifford, White, Paul and Vallotton, Annie, *Using the Bible for Reading Out Loud*. Bible Society, 1980.

Fitzsimmons, John H. and Kelly, Robert, *Being a Reader*, Kevin Mayhew, 1986.

Fitzsimmons, John H., *Guide to the Lectionary*, Mayhew-McCrimmon, 1981.

Koplik, W. J. and Brady, Joan, *Celebrating Forgiveness*, Twenty-third Publications, 1986. (Fifteen Penance celebrations.)

Sayers, Susan, *Focus the Word*, Kevin Mayhew. (Three volumes of the resources for worship based on readings for the Roman Catholic liturgy.)

Celebrating the Word, St Thomas More Pastoral Centre. (Several volumes covering the texts for Sunday Readings from the Roman Lectionary with notes on how to present the passage and suggestions for prayer.)

Baker, Thomas and Ferrone, Frank, *Liturgy Committee Basics*. St Thomas More Pastoral Centre. (A practical handbook for liturgy groups.)

With adults

Handing on the Faith in the House, Veritas Family Resources, 1980.

Bausch, W., *Storytelling: Imagination and Faith*, Twenty-third Publications, 1987.

Bishop, Anne and Hay, Eldon, *Telling My Story, Sharing My Faith*, United Church of Canada Division of Mission (85 St Clair Avenue East, Toronto, Ontario, M4T 1M8, Canada).

Manternacy, J. and Pfiefer, C., *Creative Catechist: A Comprehensive Illustrated Guide for Training Religion Teachers*, Twenty-third Publications, 1986.

Murphy, Celine and Fewell, Michael, *RICA: the Process*, T. Shand Publications, 1986.

Curtin, R., *et al, RCIA — A Practical Approach to Christian Initiation for adults*, T. Shand Publications, 1986.

Six discussion meetings for small groups. Grail Publications, 1970. (Out of print.)

Children and young people

Bible Reading Fellowship Ladder Books.

First Steps to Faith (for young people), Bible Society, 1979. (Out of print.) (Designed for anyone wanting to find out about Faith, but includes useful ideas suitable to young people.)

Young, Graham, *Bodybuilding Classes*, Bible Society, 1984. (Out of print.) (Book's range is all ages, but contains good resources for young people.)

Furnish, Dorothy Jean, *Exploring the Bible with Children*, Abingdon Press.

Griggs, Donald L., *Using the Bible in Teaching*, Bible Society, 1980.

Hall, David B., *Using the Bible with Children*, Bible Society, 1983.

Visual material and drama

Stickley, Steve and Janet and Belben, Jim, *Using the Bible in Drama*, Bible Society, 1981.

Hodgson, John and Richards, Ernest, *Improvisation*, Eyre Methuen.

Turner, James C., *Voice and Speech in the Theatre*, Pitman: Black, 1977.

Burbridge, Paul and Watts, Murray, *Time to Act*, Hodder and Stoughton, 1979.

Cotterall, Peter, *What Next?*, Lakeland. (Out of print.)

Belben, Jim and Cooper, Trevor, *Everyone's a Winner*, Bible Society, 1987. (13 games, simulations, role-plays.)

Clowney, Paul, *Picture it!*, Bible Society, 1987. (On using artistic gifts to communicate message of Scripture.)

Lamont, Gordon and Ronni, *Move Yourselves*, Bible Society, 1983. (11 workshops in music, mime and dance.)

Smith, Judy G., *Show Me!*, Bible Society, 1985. (For 3–13 year olds; includes 30 scripts.)

For filmstrips and slide productions:
The Church Army, Church Army Headquarters, Independents Road, London SE23 9LG.

For the hire of films:
Concordia Films, Viking Way, Bar Hill Village, Cambridge, CB3 0EL.

For videos:
Veritas Video, Veritas House, 7–8 Lower Abbey Street, Dublin 1.

For posters:
Argus posters. Available from Argus Communications, DLM House, Edinburgh Way, Harlow, Essex CM20 2HL.
Palm Tree posters. Available from Palm Tree Press Ltd, Rattlesden, Bury St Edmunds, Suffolk IP30 0SZ.

Many posters and visual material can also be obtained from agencies such as CAFOD and Christian Aid.

Useful addresses

The Bible Reading Fellowship, St Michael's House, 2 Elizabeth Street, London SW1W 9RQ.
(Produces Bible notes for individual use, children and young people's notes, as well as some study group material.)

Bible Society, Stonehill Green, Westlea, Swindon SN5 7DG.
(Produces Bible study resources for adults, young people and children and distributes Bibles throughout the world.)

The Catholic Biblical Association, 1 Malcolm Road, Wimbledon, London SW19.

Family and Social Action, 120B West Heath Road, London NW3 7TY.
(Produces material for small groups, with particular emphasis on social questions.)

The Grail Publications, 125 Waxwell Lane, Pinner, Middlesex HA5 3ER.

The Scripture Union, 130 City Road, London EC1V 2NJ.
(An Evangelical organisation with a huge range of resources including visual and audio-visual material.)

St Thomas More Pastoral Centre, The Burroughs, Hendon, London NW4 4TY.
(Produces resources for liturgy.)

Veritas Family Resources, 44 Rathfriland Road, Newry, Co. Down BT34 1LD.
(Produces a pre-Baptism preparation programme and parenting programme.)